D1006651

JOHANNES BOBROWSKI

MODERN GERMAN AUTHORS

TEXTS AND CONTEXTS

Ed. R. W. Last

VOLUME FOUR

JOHANNES BOBROWSKI

by

BRIAN KEITH-SMITH

WITH FOUR ILLUSTRATIONS

by

Fritz Möser

OSWALD WOLFF

London

1970

MODERN GERMAN AUTHORS—Texts and Contexts
ed. R. W. Last

ISBN 0 85496 044 9

© Oswald Wolff (Publishers) Limited, London, 1970

MADE AND PRINTED IN GREAT BRITAIN BY
THE GARDEN CITY PRESS LIMITED
LETCHWORTH, HERTFORDSHIRE

CONTENTS

ACKNOWLEDGEMENTS

My thanks are due to my colleague Mr. Stanley Radcliffe and to Mr. Michael Shiels for reading some of my translations and offering most helpful advice; also to Professor H. M. Waidson for sending me a draft of his article on *Levins Mühle*; and also to the following publishers for permission to use copyright material: Deutsche Verlags-Anstalt, Stuttgart; Rapp & Whiting, London; Union Verlag, Berlin; Klaus Wagenbach, Berlin. The illustrations by Fritz Möser from his cycle of linocuts *Das Land Sarmatien* appear by kind permission of Frau Hildegard Modlmayr.

Most of all I should like to thank those of my Heidelberg friends with whom I discussed Bobrowski's work and to whom I offer this volume as a small token of gratitude—in particular to Herrn and Frau Modlmayr, Herrn Schneider, Dr. and Frau Wezzel; and, finally, to Anne-Marie, my wife.

FRITZ MOSER—A BIOGRAPHICAL NOTE

Fritz Möser was born in 1932 in Bensen (Czecho-
slovakia) where his father owned a printing works. A
skilled printer and typesetter, Fritz Möser now lives
in Memmingen (Bavaria). His first linocuts were
completed in 1958. After illustrating countless books
he has produced cycles of graphic works, water
colours and monotypes.

His works have been exhibited so far in the
following towns: Hanover (1965), Füssen (1965–
1968), Berlin (1966, 1967–1968), Mestre/Venice
(1967), Heidelberg (1967–1968), Munich (1968),
Memmingen (1968), Karlsruhe (1968–1969), Göt-
tingen (1968), Gelsenkirchen-Buer (1969).

His most important cycles of lino-cuts are:

Totentanz	10 sheets	40 copies sold out
Ballett in Linol	11 sheets	45 copies sold out
Primavera I	5 sheets	40 copies
Orfeo 66	28 sheets	100 copies
Primavera II	15 sheets	100 copies
Bibel AT	33 sheets	50 copies
Golgatha Fragment	8 sheets	40 copies
Das Land Sarmatien für		
Johannes Bobrowski	9 sheets	45 copies
Die Offenbarung des		
Johannes	10 sheets	75 copies

NOTE

Numbers in brackets in the mono-
graph refer to the translations in the
second part of the volume.

MONOGRAPH

LIFE AND WORKS

It is not often that a writer whose publications only include two novels, some 170 poems, about forty shorter prose pieces and a few epigrams and short notes, is recognised within five years of his death at the age of forty-eight on at least a European scale as one of the most individual and most important literary voices of our times. And it is rare to find a German writer of today who is welcome apparently for similar reasons on both sides of the Iron Curtain, yet whose work and figure has become a legend in an age scornful or scared of ideals seemingly irrelevant to the urgent demands of modern life. Bobrowski's individuality and humanity cut across all artificial boundaries—however real and harsh they may seem—and speak with the voice of another age, an age and landscape whose slow pace and natural contours seem at first idyllic or even an escape from contemporary reality. Yet although Bobrowski is generally mentioned as a 'nature-poet', it is clear that his comprehension and portrayal of natural landscape is primarily a lament to man's estrangement from it and thus from his fellow creatures.

Bobrowski's life and environment made him aware from the first of the sharp contrasts between different ethnic types, mixed languages and dialects, village tradition and mature provincial urban culture, the cycle of agricultural economy and the urge for change in the growth of commercial and industrial power. Born in 1917 the son of a railway official in Tilsit, a local central town in East Prussia on the river Memel and close to the Lithuanian frontier, Bobrowski spent much of his boyhood in his grandparents' village homes closer still to the frontier. There was a mixed population of Germans, Lithuanians, Poles and Russians, all retaining their customs and beliefs, and markedly influenced by a large Jewish element.

Later Bobrowski was to call the main theme of his writing an act of atonement for the long history of oppression practised by the Germans from the days of the Teutonic Knights into the most recent past. That his stories in particular portray for the most part a form of local human justice which is earthy and at times rather harsh reflects the unengaged essential character of communities built up for generations out of innate hostility yet mutual respect. It is this factor of mutual respect, shown to be far more active than mere tolerance, that enables the reader to view Bobrowski's village tales as a theatre of the world in miniature. It is a quality which consists in not glossing over individual weaknesses and cruelties, but in recognising them, naming them, exorcising them as it were. For Bobrowski this implies that no state system, whether religious, ideological or locally political, can possibly fit the individual. This positive impartiality (see *Mouse banquet* (24)) is doubtless one of the reasons why Bobrowski's works appeal in both East and West, why in particular they are more readily acceptable to younger readers whose views have not been set into moulds cast by the direct experience of war and tyranny.

In 1928 Bobrowski moved with his family to Königsberg, whose renowned literary and musical past and fame as the place where Hamann and Kant had lived continued as a lively tradition in its academies and societies (see the story *Der Mahner*). Here he learnt in particular to appreciate the form and discipline of classical Greek and Latin writers and to play the organ and clavichord. He developed a taste for Baroque music, for Bach, Buxtehude and Mozart. Above all he experienced the sharp contrast between, as he put it, the patriarchal closed-inness of village life and the sophisticated worldly preoccupations of a trading port with a proud cultural past. If we want to understand the cultural influences which Bobrowski particularly favoured, it is to the traditions of Königsberg that we must turn—to the world of the *Aufklärung* and the *Strum und Drang*; to Hamann's belief in poetry as the mother-language of the human race; to Klopstock's enthusiasm for the classical and biblical expression of man's relationship with the gods of the landscape; and to Herder's visions of a time when man would free himself of ancient restrictions on his creative spirit.

Later Bobrowski would collect many of their works in their original editions alongside specialist studies on the geography and history of the region. It is interesting to note that, among the works he edited as a publisher's reader towards the end of his life, were Gustav Schwab's *Die schönsten Sagen des klassischen Altertums*, the same writer's adaptations of the sagas of Troy and Odysseus' homecoming, an anthology of eighteenth-century love-poems, Jean Paul's *Leben Fibels* and a delightful children's book of animal stories which he adapted from the Russian original. In his story *Looking at a picture* (22), he refers to some of the many travel books and atlases which deeply interested him. These interests, coupled with the later training he would temporarily have as a student of art-history for a year before the outbreak of war, gave him a peculiarly balanced combination of close attachment to the significance of local life, where the quality of the individual character and his expression meant so much, and of the detachment of an observer with a developed taste for the strict form of some of the highest achievements of classical post-Renaissance and ancient classical culture.

Bobrowski's characters in his works have some of this double existence—they are held in the bounds of their often pitifully narrow existence, yet display an openness to the world and in particular to unfamiliar cultural values that makes of them proud and often eccentric individuals and at the same time mentors of mankind in general. That they should be so is partly a direct result of Bobrowski's own upbringing and education, but also supports the claim made in his address in December 1962 to the Evangelical Academy of Berlin-Brandenburg (*Benannte Schuld-gebannte Schuld?*) that the writer has to deal with man in the 10,000th year of history. He has to be addressed personally, but the full force of his cultural and political heritage has to be taken into account. Bobrowski's writings reveal both this direct personal quality and deep traces of age-old cultural traditions about them. With this in mind we can understand why it was Bobrowski's hope to write a major work on Hamann, and why his poem in tribute to Hamann tries to bring together the worlds of culture and natural landscape in a personal and representative manner.

The earliest writings of Bobrowski—apparently autobiographical sketches—seem to have been lost. As a schoolboy he corresponded with Ina Seidel, was a friend of the poet Alfred Brust, and was taught Latin by the Christian writer Ernst Wiechert. Since 1938 his family has lived in Berlin-Friedrichshagen where he began his studies of art history and became particularly interested in the German Baroque. Called up in 1939 he was first sent to Poland (see the stories *Der Tänzer Malige* and *Mouse banquet* (24), later into Russia where he began to write poetry (*Lake Ilmen 1941* (3), *Invocation* (1), *The Don* (15), etc.). In captivity until 1949 he tried to capture the essence of the Russian landscape first in drawings, then in short prose sketches and finally in the alchaic and sapphic ode forms of Klopstock and Hölderlin. His most important poems were written as a publisher's reader from 1952 (until 1959 with the Berlin Verlag Lucie Groszer, for whom he edited in particular a small book on *Hans Clauert, der märkische Eulenspiegel,* and later with Union Verlag) until 1963. They first appeared in periodicals, not until 1961 as the collection *Sarmatische Zeit* and in 1962 *Schattenland Ströme* in book form. Only one short piece of prose had been published by him before 1962, and the novels *Levins Mühle* and *Litauische Claviere* appeared in 1964 and 1966. Eventually, no doubt, the significant letters he wrote will also be published—the short correspondence with Paul Celan would be of particular interest, but as far as is known, no complete work of his still remains unpublished.

Bobroswki's last few years were spent relatively quietly: he carefully avoided any direct political activity, yet his growing recognition and calm voice were much respected by writers and intellectuals in both the East and the West. His complete self-effacement in his public life and his poetry was an act of deep sincerity that mistrusted experiment and was determined to come to terms with the lessons of the past. Perhaps it was because his work ran deeper and closer to the heart of man than so much of the cerebral, anxiety-ridden expressions of contemporary poetry, that it was acclaimed by the Gruppe 47 among others as a refreshing and much-needed draught of commonsense humanity. He died in 1965 from peritonitis just as his works were beginning to receive the acclaim of a much wider audience than his previously small circle of admirers.

In claiming that his central theme was an act of atonement, Bobrowski hinted at the essentially narrative quality of much of his prose and poetry. It is largely this that determines the usually free rhythms and structures of his poetry, yet we are never allowed to forget for long the haunting presence of stricter measures. The musical quality of his poetry, sometimes based on traditional folksong melodies (see *Village music* (19)) and sometimes on the fugal structure (see *J. S. Bach*), can even be found extended into an intricate prose work like *D.B.H.* based on a Buxtehude composition. By contrast there are such works as *Looking at a picture* (22) or *Im Guckkasten: Galiani* where it is the painter rather than the musician who narrates, others such as *Report* (5), *Barlach in Güstrow* (17) and *Gedenkblatt* which are directly inspired by the searing quality of a photograph. In these, as indeed in the attitudes towards life and other people of most of the characters whom

Bobrowski clearly portrays with sympathy, there is an element of experiment, an attempt to renarrate other experiences as a form of enjoyment or warning for oneself. Thus it is that the sub-title of *Levins Mühle* is *Vierunddreißig Sätze über meinen Großvater*—an attempt to define the world of the narrator's grandfather in order to find out and expiate his actions; thus it is that *Litauische Claviere* is the story of two musicians' attempts to glean enough local colour and information about a legendary figure to be able to write a German-Lithuanian opera, and bring the two races together by means of this exemplary character. In both novels certain standards of human performance are continually referred to and the individual judged against these, whether as policeman, circus artiste, teacher or singer. The admiration for craftsmanship is marked both in the characters Bobrowski created and in the carefully written terse style he developed as a writer of lyric and prose.

2

POETIC CRAFTSMANSHIP

There are various features of Bobrowski's craftsmanship which characterise in general terms both his lyric poetry and his prose. He had a marked ability to form original, often multi-dimensional images. As a musician he was especially careful with the counterpoint of rhythmic movement. He exercised an individual ordering of phrases and lines within the sentence and verse. Above all, he learnt how to combine clearly several poetic devices at once to bring about a precise effect. He could achieve variety through changes in tone—often unexpected but always relevant, and which sometimes reveal the poet's own gesture towards his material. A particularly marked feature of this was his use of humour. His accuracy in historical allusion and local details often leads to suggestions of whole worlds of saga and myth. For all the disciplined use of language and poetic form, the atmosphere and settings of much of his poetry are sunlit with the self-contained yet knowingly restricted rough-and-tumble of country village life. This is especially true of his novels, where the social factor is most important. The intricate inner patterns of his lyrics are often governed by the weather, the seasons and time-cycles that are particularly insistent in country life. There is, too, an attractive outer simplicity in Bobrowski's lyrics which parallels the directness of dialogue and speech. In fact use of the second person is frequent. Set in a fierce landscape with huge plains, great rivers and deep forests where a primitive elemental religion and the force of superstition are very strong, Bobrowski's poetry is at times harsh and unrelenting. Yet its tone is mainly subdued, reticent, sober, and rarely touched with sentimentality. Its diction is outstanding for its richly allusive quality, its lyrical and rhythmical strength and austere compactness. One feels that the interdependence of poetic device—of meaning, local figurative connotation, rhythmical quality, tone, vowel and consonantal interplay, and syntactical freedom—is most intricately enmeshed. Yet, when read, the poems run off in such a decided and clear manner that one is left with the false impression that their language and vision is restricted, their appeal local and discriminatory. They are delicately balanced somewhere between almost colloquial narrative and metaphysical abstractness. It is that quality perhaps that comes closest and most compellingly to their underlying theme that man can upset the intricate calibration of the natural landscape and cast a shadow over it for generations to come. At times this attains a haunting quality in which a synthesis of visual and aural elements plays a large part—thus for instance in *Das Holzhaus über der Wilia* where the fixation of different shades of darkness and light is recalled by reference to bird song and poetic invocation. The old house, so much a living thing and centre of a whole landscape of life, can only be recaptured by the poet through a process of throwing away normal self-centred life, as a girl throws over her shoulder a garland in the hope that someone will pick it up. Such a gesture is a typical linking motif in Bobrowski's poetry, and reveals the separateness and closeness of two worlds. The house Bobrowski invokes is on the shadow-edge of the woods, is set in the 'Flußwald', and lies on the border between light and darkness. Much of his poetry explores such a region. In doing so it immediately suggests the closeness of man to nature, claims attention to the force of the irrational, and above all seeks to reinstate the creativity of language as a revealer of irrational natural forces as opposed to rational abstractions. In different ways we find this expressed in such poems as *Tree nymph* (9), *Invocation* (1), *Pruzzian elegy* (2), and *Always to be named* (7).

Perhaps one of the most characteristic of Bobrowski's poems is *Dead language* (6). In it, he captures the traditional relationship between man and the landscape, and its expression in the Old Prussian language. Old Prussian was one of the Baltic languages that retained many features of Indo-European and existed side by side with Lithuanian and Lettish, until in the thirteenth century the Teutonic knights virtually extinguished it by the introduction of German. By 1677 there is supposed to have been only one speaker of Prussian left in the district, but the traditions which it expressed remained in local custom and beliefs. Its only other significant expression as a cultural influence and historical background is to be found in some of the dramas of Zacharias Werner and in the stories and ballads of Agnes Miegel. An academic interest in the language and in its folk religious practices lingers on from the revival of local enquiries in the nineteenth century and in the researches of Reinhold Trautmann in the first quarter of the twentieth century and of Werner Maser in recent years.

In Bobrowski's poem the basic proofs of life—movement, utterance, growth, reproduction, and decay—are set in a framework which makes use of connecting elements: 'Bogen' and 'Fluß' ('bow' and 'stream'). Yet none of these reach meaningful existence in themselves. The active use is needed of a language whose implications and sense of human commitment to the landscape express the life of a reality that has died together with its mode of expression. The two languages—German and Old Prussian—coexist in this poem and represent two different worlds. German here is the language of narration and half-realisation of the reality of the situation. Old Prussian is the voice of the challenge which nature's laws present, of myth, and of the tragic consequences should man ignore them. The title does not specify which of the two is dead: is Old Prussian dead because it is not heeded, or German dead because it here no longer expresses the 'brotherhood' of man and nature? Or can the title refer to the death of the poetic powers of evocation in both when they are separated? The Old Prussian 'Laurio' has to be reinterpreted, its qualities spelt out in four German synonyms. The significance of 'Warne' and 'Wittan' has to be translated and used as an explicit analogy to develop the present situation. The word 'smordis' is no longer immediately charged with enough foreboding, is not at once comprehended ('verstanden'), but gathered ('vernommen'), and its threat has to be translated with rhythmical and syntactical devices to help in full detail. But the German too, by itself, needs the support of the world expressed by the Old Prussian for the narrated event in order to gain full poetic meaning. Thus, for example, 'die Krähe hat keinen Baum' ('the crow it has no tree') can only be understood in its full force when it is brought into poetic connection with 'ich wohne in deinem Ohr' ('I dwell in your listening ear'). One of the central features of the old Prussian folk religion was the dependence of the family's fortunes on the health of the tree in which dwelt their protective spirit. This found its way into North German phrases about the tree of one's life growing green or withering away. The protective spirit would often take the form of a bird which would fly away when its tree was dying. The birds and their behaviour—and Bobrowski makes frequent use of them in his poetry—are an immediate and important pointer to the individual's fate, and their homes in trees signs of the health of the family's

23

fortune. Without Old Prussian's background of allusion, the modern German is less directly poetic; without the explanation of modern German, the Old Prussian forgotten language is no longer comprehensible. In bringing together the two languages in his poem, Bobrowski has revitalised both and, at the same time, suggested the need for brotherhood. Drawing on old forms, he has produced an original expression of what may sound a hackneyed theme, and has managed through the personal direct approach and appeal to the insistence of life's claims to produce a freshness that remains on re-reading.

3

MYTHOLOGY AND LOCAL TRADITION

Bobrowski's invocation in many of his works of the Balto-Slav mythology is only partly an attempt to recreate the Prussian folklore virtually destroyed by the Teutonic Order in the thirteenth and fourteenth centuries in the name of the Roman Catholic Church. It is an essential element of the psychological make-up of a mixed race that lives on in superstition, tradition, names, etc. (see *Pruzzian elegy* (2)), and it is part of Bobrowski's achievement to have made the particular Prussian background archetypal enough for it to be accepted as a general statement on man the oppressor and man the sufferer throughout the ages. The Gods and hero-figures that he evokes exercise a fascination on the minds of his characters and, it would seem, on the poet himself. That is in itself a proof of his detachment from the ideological confrontations of the twentieth century. These ancient forces are one indication of the antirational impulse that informs his understanding of the landscape in which he was brought up and from whose power he never really escaped, nor perhaps wanted to escape. More than a link with the past, they became for him both a threat to man's freedom from traditional taboos and fears, but also at times an escape from the harsh realities of the twentieth-century reliance on an apparently man-made world.

Bobrowski's attachment to the world of mythology betrays an essential conservatism and respect for well-tried values, for proven valour and wisdom, and sympathy for anyone who lives according to the age-old demands of life, one is almost inclined to say, according to some natural law—however harsh it may be against the individual—rather than according to some revolutionary theory for the future. Bobrowski's religiosity is basically pagan, conditioned as it is by the forces that have held sway in the landscape and among the people from which he came. The pre-Christian mythology was based on a religion whose central place of worship was the ancient oak Romove in which a statue of Perkunas its supreme God was placed. Other gods such as Pikollo (Old Prussian pickuls = devil, golis = death, and also known as Patollo: Old Prussian pa-tolus = underworld), Potrymbus (Potrimpo = the corn spirit), Perkuno the god of thunder (like the Russian Pjerun, the supreme thunder-god), Kurcho the harvest god, and Lauma the hag all held their place in a cult presided over by the sage Kirwaïto.

It is to such a heritage that Bobrowski sings. Sometimes this can be insistent (see *Dead language* (6)), or can refer to specific historical events as in the poem *An Nelly Sachs* and in the story *Die Seligkeit der Heiden*, which narrates the casting into the river Dnieper of the great oak in 988. One senses the fear of change from the pagan ritual to the new Christian one, the recoiling from the destruction of a world whose values had been formative for generations of local people and from the forcible grafting on to them of an outside culture. Strongly sympathetic for all that is creative in man, Bobrowski was filled with lament and anger for the destructive impulse, for the attainment of one's goal by force. But his oppressed characters are not made into ideals of moral or human behaviour—the hero in his works is nearly always a mythical figure of the past, and is celebrated more for efficiency than for qualities of leadership. Indeed the only true heroism in Bobrowski's land-scapes is that of life itself—a form of resignation rather than triumph (see, for example, *Letter from America* (23)). There is an instinctive withdrawal from all the manifestations of power—the hunter-figure, the bird of prey, the wolf, the unknown stran-ger—and yet he is fascinated by their presence, and loves the order which they bring into the landscape. Thus, like Stifter's mountains, Bobrowski's rivers lend it the necessary bounds and contours, beyond which lies not a challenge but the unknown. To answer a call to conquer the unknown would be almost an unnatural and thus undignified act. Bobrowski's world is not idyllic, but it is one in which life's main business is an act of acclimatisation to its order and its harshness. Man, Bobrowski sees, is born neither to appease nor to conquer, but to coexist with the forces of nature around him.

However, coexistence implies full realisation of the lessons from the past. Forgetfulness, as we see in the poem *Elder blossom* (4), may even become destructive. The significant feature of the poem is the complete lack of any direct comment on the events of the pogrom, allowing that word itself to colour over all the landscape that remains. However hard we may attempt to scrub out or forget the past, the bloodstain remains. No attempt to explain the pogrom away, no comment on it is sufficient—not even one of horror. All the poet apparently does is to sum up in Isaak Babel's memory the significant happening of the pogrom as it affected him. To have dwelt on the cruelty, the meaninglessness, the inhumanity of the act of tearing the pigeon's head off would have drawn away the attention from the contrasting motif of the neat village street with its elder bushes. Life finds new modes of expression, but while Isaak Babel remains (his name itself, referring also to the Jewish poet, is presented impersonally as if on some register, and may imply both confusion and sacrifice), the bloodstain has meaning, is not just a red spot, and is not as yet described as such. The third motif is that of the threat to the renewal of life itself. The laughter of forgetfulness or of not knowing can only be an injury to the elder bushes, for they will no longer have purpose in the neat village street, but will be replaced as central focus of attention by the aimless laughter. Such aimlessness will be shown up as self-indulgence for all its innocence if the elder dies. The parents have the responsibility of training the youngsters— just to train the elder bushes is not in itself enough.

Order in life, and in particular the continuance of its creativity, depends on a full acceptance and passing-on of lessons learnt from, or at least a recording of the events of, the past. Man left to the whims of self-indulgence can become inhumanly self-destructive of living things, and reacts with what looks like almost a fetish for order and cleanliness, and, by trying to forget, merely allows his next generation to behave as mirror images of that artificial order without explaining what it stands for. Left with no explanation, the new generation unwittingly threatens to start the whole cycle again. The structure of the poem also bears this out, for Isaak Babel is clearly an outsider—he is neither spoken to, nor does he seem at all closely connected to, the narrator. The force of the narrative 'He says' suggests a repeated story to which the narrator does not react any more. There is almost a jolt of unexpected reminiscence at the end of the second verse : 'But then, remember, the bloodstain' as if the poet has turned away from Isaak Babel and lost himself in contemplating the tidiness of the village, only to be reminded yet again of the bloodstain. In the third verse the poet turns to active exhortation, to insistent counter-cries to the indifference of the 'people'.

The poem becomes more attractive when we think of the traditional associations connected with the elder tree. For across the whole range of Slavonic legend the elder was respected and almost worshipped for its powers of healing and prophecy. And in folk poetry it stands for marriage and sexual love (thus from Holunder = elder tree, we find the phrase 'Hollermade' for girls who lose their virginity before marriage). A typical example of a whole tradition is the Polish folksong *Father and Mother have gone to Krakau*, where the girl first of all symbolically plucks elder blossom and almost automatically seems to be able to offer rest and refreshment to horse and rider, and finally herself to the passing stranger. Bringing such knowledge to bear on Bobrowski's poetry frequently opens up further levels of interpretation, and indeed no full understanding of it can be made without reference to this traditional folklore background and the typical human activities associated with it. It is Bobrowski's particular quality as a poet that he knew how to write arresting lyrics that for the most part have a clear message of their own to anyone who still reacts to the clear-cut values of life on a village scale, and where the petty grievances and dealings of the day are underpinned by hazy legends and knowledge of the remote past. At the same time he makes use of local colour that gives his poetry an air of folk-song in formal literary dress. There could be nothing worse perhaps than a phony-sounding folk-poet, whose structural devices are used as an artificial mould for traditional themes and figures, but Bobrowski usually managed to keep clear of that danger. His instinctive love of the simple in life and his highly trained musical ear was coupled with a blend of humorous disbelief in the ultimate seriousness of culture for its own sake.

4

LIFE IN LANDSCAPE

Bobrowski had too the qualities of a visionary. This is seen for instance in his many river poems. The awe and seriousness with which he considered rivers are only one part of his poetic personality, but at times this seems overwhelmingly important to him. The Don, for example, was probably the most Eastern river Bobrowski knew, yet although he first encountered it as a prisoner of war, that fact alone did not make it into a spiritual frontier for him.

In the poem *The Don* (15), the river is seen as a natural frontier whose presence recast the roles of different parts of the landscape. The cry of the Div (presumably eastwards across the plains and westwards into the hills) seems to be a cry of warning from a borderland, from a landscape peopled by the dead. It is a strangely monumental landscape marked out by violent contrasts—thus the whiteness of the river emphasising the darkness of the higher banks, the villages built high up (for strategic reasons like, for example, the *villages perchés* in Provence, seen either from the river against the setting sun and thus as if on fire, or so often changing hands that they had become almost literally villages of fire. The permanent quality of the first sentence in the poem with no verb seems to ridicule the haste of the second, and it is fully complemented by the threat of cold and darkness in the third. The collapse from the heights and burning villages down to the freezing darkness of the river that can only breathe icily and cannot move suggests most vividly an apocalyptic landscape (to be compared with the one described in the poem *Icon* (13)). It is a compact vision of destruction to almost total entropy told with a variety of syntactical devices that is the mark of a post-expressionist poet or painter. Yet the alliterative force of the stressed syllables, which in the German begin with 'f', and the strongly-tensed rhythmical structure remind one of Old High

German or, as is more relevant here, Old Russian forms. Here, as in the poem *Singschwan*, Bobrowski refers to the Russian *Igor* saga, and not a little of its terse structure has been recaptured in his poems. In the second verse the contrasts of dark and light, of plain and hill, of level fields and towering walls stand out. Out of the permanence of the white frozen river and the mysterious dark banks struggles the image of climbing horses; suddenly the banks fly away, as if the poet's vision has unexpectedly cleared, and distant walls are seen.

In a way this is the image of the whole essence of Bobrowski's poetry. Out of contrast and the apparent permanence of the present landscape Bobrowski has created images that release the hidden significance of that landscape. His images are creative vectors that link up again individual parts of the landscape whose interrelationships man had destroyed or forgotten or neglected for so long that he had lost contact with them at all but superficial levels. Bobrowski's voice is like that of the Div commanding plains and hills, calling back features from the past, filling the landscape once again with the struggling forces that once gave it its character. The river and its immediate surroundings have become a challenge to reinstate the past. The landscape is shown to contain forces that can commit man or pattern his existence provided someone—whether Div or poet—is there to point this out.

Seen from this angle, it is understandable why Bobrowski is one of the rare examples of an East German poet in the twentieth century to write and publish dedicatory poems beyond the limitations of party propaganda, and which are formal attempts to

express the essence of a completely alien way of life
and thought. Bobrowski's dozen or so poems that
celebrate major literary figures all refer to the closeness of the writer to landscape, many indeed to the
meaning-giving power each writer's voice has to his
own or to another landscape. Bobrowski's contribu-
tion, for example, to German literary interest in
Thomas Chatterton is marked with traditional literary knowledge while at the same time emphasising
the particular relationship between Chatterton and
the landscape into which he was born and in which
he lived and died.

Ode to Thomas Chatterton (18) joins Ernst Penzoldt's biographical novel and Hans Henny Jahnn's
tragedy in celebrating Bristol's poet. Its form makes it
one of the few outstanding examples of the Sapphic
ode in twentieth-century German literature. As it is
necessary to know about traditional folklore in order
to understand such a poem as *Elder blossom* (4), so
one should have some previous knowledge of Chatterton's life and of the Bristol landscape in order fully to
understand Bobrowski's ode. In fact it is clear from
several details that Bobrowski relied on Penzoldt's
book rather than on a personal knowledge of his
subject. The reliance on legend need not blunt the
effectiveness of Bobrowski's purpose, for his careful
selection of details aims to reawaken an atmosphere,
a whole world, appealing because of its remoteness,
yet strangely close in its revelation of intimate human
anxieties.

The concision of Bobrowski's opening description
of St. Mary Redcliffe, its sudden imperturbable
Gothic presence and the mellifluous interplay of direct, varied yet simple grammatical constructions,

vowel sounds, and open-ended rhythmical patterns, is in itself a poetic *tour de force*. The gravedigger episode is biographically accurate, as is Chatterton's use of pseudonyms, and both appear in Penzoldt's novel. The insistent negatives leading to Chatterton's despair turn into a more general reflection on poetic inspiration and creation, which for all its growth cannot hide despair. Here the examination of a particular poet's difficulties is gently turned into exemplary statements for man in general. One can hardly miss the parallel between the description of the foliage growing out of everyday experience and that of St. Mary Redcliffe growing out of the past yet still seemingly alive through its 'walls ... trickling with shadows'. The shadows thrown by the tree are as unavoidable, yet as unhelpful as those of the church. The poet, in fleeing the shadows out from the town to the surrounding countryside by the river banks until the morning dew, does not escape; nor does he in other towns. Nature has an implacable indifference of its own in Bobrowski's poetry. Chatterton's tragedy is non-acceptance as a poet in the human world, but also an immaturity that cannot accept resignation to the forces of time, loneliness, obscurity, nonentity. Relentlessly and dramatically, life takes its toll on Chatterton's frenzied search for absolute experience in London. Death comes as a medieval figure with the ironic naming of the pseudonym 'Rowley' and the hero-figure 'Aella'—both signs of Chatterton's sense of insecurity and lack of self-confidence. The poem emphasises him as a child, as immature and alone—his poetry grows as a foliage apart from and apparently useless to its author.

Through his celebration of Chatterton we may

well see that Bobrowski was carrying out the necessary poetic task of self-effacement. His ode becomes, like so many of his works, at once a lament and a warning, a lesson and a personal victory. It has most fittingly been called a secular psalm, and is a poem whose form and language emphasise the tension between the poet Chatterton's instinctive feelings and his growing self-knowledge and self-detachment. As so often in Bobrowski's works, there is an immediate, almost automatic transition from passive impression to active expression—thus the sudden image of the tree.

5

POETIC PATTERNS

The suddenness of Bobrowski's images, often reinforced by deliberate heavily marked caesuras and turns in the rhythmic patterns of the lines, lends his poetry a sense of actuality and dramatic presence. A single word can highlight an event and radiate meaning throughout the poem at different levels. An obvious example is 'pogrom' in *Elder blossom* (4). The repeated entry of the wolf in *Lake Ilmen 1941* (3) catches the double aspect of that poem : the pinpoint accuracy of time and place in the poet's experience of the lake, and the endless drawn-out effect of that place and its expression through the howling wolf. Many of Bobrowski's poems begin abruptly. Needing no verb or adjectival explanation, they present the general picture or atmosphere of a landscape in one or a few nouns. Many of them end rhetorically either as a challenge or as a harsh statement of reality. Often the word that most fully explains the poem comes late in the final section, and the reader is forced to unravel its implications back through the poem as someone in reality would reinterpret events from hindsight (e.g. *Kalmus* (10), where the 'green sword' refers back to the plant of the title). This has an important function in the whole purpose of Bobrowski's poetry, for, as with Klopstock, Bobrowski believed in poetry as a moral force. The carefully adapted traditional forms and reflection back over the event are a call for man to linger and live out a life of fuller meaning, rather than merely being carried along from event to event. Thus we find continual reference to the father-figure as a source of wisdom (see the novels, the story *Mouse banquet* (24) and the poem *Invocation* (1)). Thus too the suggestions that man has forgotten, and the poet can only name, sketch and colour (see *Always to be named* (7)).

Reality is thereby reinstated as a non-selective objective force, for Bobrowski managed at times to portray it in terms of its colour and dynamic force, and as an expression of undeniable natural patterns. He refuses to accept it as a series of unconnected subjective impressions. He finds man unworthy to stand at the centre of the landscape, but seeks out for him a role within its various modes of expression. These modes are for ever shifting, just as the pace and direction of many of Bobrowski's poems do. Some of the vast spaces of the landscapes in which many of them are set seem to have been caught in the controlled freedom of their inner structure and meaning.

This technique has been excellently summed-up in the anonymous review of *Schattenland Ströme* in the *Times Literary Supplement* as follows :

> Rhythms then so arrange the phrases that, inside the dominant very slow trochaic or dactylic patterns, accents fall serially on different parts of speech. In German, inflected forms add to the variety of zestful verbal gesture so arranged. Longish lacunae occur, where several unaccented syllables form a silence of the breath. A double counterpoint is established : the word alone connotes the cosmos of its ideal relations; meanwhile the rhythm proceeding dwells, over and over, on one word or on a small verbless whirl of words which is then resolved back into the rhythmic procession as a fresh finite verb carries the thrust of speech forward. Each poem is a crosswork of halt and thrust, of singularity and complicity. . . . This procedure integrates lyric and dramatic kinds of perception.

In other words, Bobrowski uses a form of sprung rhythm irregularly fitted to the amount of emphasis found in the expression of any feature or event in the landscape. This is a form of relative freedom within the overall classical patterns (see *In the stream* (14), *The Don* (15), *Russian songs* (12), *Tree nymph* (9), etc.) which depends mainly on the particular genius of the German language. It is this that makes Bobrowski's work—whether poetry or prose—sound so musical. His landscapes are real in the sense that they are readily identifiable with particular geographical sites, they are mythical in the sense that they are understood and described as rhythmical expressions. They are given their own singular character, but retain a common manifestation of age-old lasting relationships between man and the gods, between the elements and different species' way of life.

A fine example of Bobrowski's combined use of various poetic devices is the poem *Pruzzian elegy* (2), which is not included in the West German editions of his poetry. The opening-out effect of the first three verses and the closing-together again in verse four in the two sentences beginning 'So . . .' catches the subjective effect brought about by childhood memories lingered over in retrospect—a re-enactment of an extended period in the past—and by the constricting narrowed vision of the present which has almost forgotten the past, save through the songs of old women and 'just a thin tinkling' of broken bells. The poet has constructed his position as an eager listner to the fullness of the past; his song becomes an act of listening. The need to listen is an important theme in Bobrowski's poetry (see *Dead language* (6), *Tree nymph* (9), *Invocation* (1), *Always to be named* (7), etc.), so often for him is the natural life-force expressed as a continuous sound. The sound is vague, lasting and often stream-like : that is, it has no precise time-location. It is an 'Anruf der Vorzeit' (a 'call from before time'), and it is the voice to which Bobrowski continually turns. Above all it is the voice which can only be expressed in human terms through the medium of music or poetry. This is because it consists primarily of movement and rhythm, is tremulous rather than percussive, but also because the development of language to rational uses has demanded a functionalisation and brevity contrary to the organic shifting quality of nature. The fifth and sixth verses of

Pruzzian elegy (2) capture remarkably the quiet incessant rhythms and endlessness of a timeless landscape (woods, rivers, haffs, and sea); the close-to-nature hunting, herding and harvesting of a people worshipping elemental gods; the complete identification of man within such a system in joy and death; and, finally, the disjointed rhythms of war and frenzy. In this pagan history of a people's development towards militarism and destruction, there is a parallel to that from the old women's songs (comparison with *Invocation* (1) shows Bobrowski's reverence for the oracular) to the broken bells. Indeed the phases of idyllic childhood, smouldering groves and death are repeated—the poet's own fate is identified with that of the people to whom he sings. The ultimate destruction of that people is averted through his naming of them, and he does this—perhaps necessarily because they have been so downtrodden—seven times. The final vision of the unknown god's mother with the allusion to the 'Son's gallows' can—but not necessarily—turn the whole poem in the direction of a specifically Judaeo-Christian context. The last verse, however, with its emphasis on lasting, moving, time-free images, specifically reinserts the song and the naming into equal partnership with direct features of the landscape, legends and the archetypal fisherman as potential revelations of the Prussian or any other oppressed people. The song has had 'its plaint made poor' ('vor Klage arm'); it was supposed to have been 'bitter with lament' ('von Klage bitter'). Bobrowski has achieved more than an old woman's song, for he has transcended lament and transferred it into an elegy. The poverty of the lament is attached to the eternal white-haired fisherman's catch. The poet has found an independence from too close an association with the graveyard world of verse four, and has found a more positive *alter ego* in the fisherman.

This image, so closely fitted into the landscape, illustrates Bobrowski's general comment on nature poetry:

> I think, that when today a lyric poet writes a poem about nature, he not only includes his own person, which in any case comes into the poem as the lyrical self, but seeks a relationship with the people who live in that nature and also form it; a landscape in which men have worked, in which men live, in which men are active.
>
> (*Neue Deutsche Literatur* XXII (1965), 135.)

Man is Bobrowski's chief concern, not as an isolated phenomenon or specimen, but set within a landscape, caught in the flow of time, committed to a confrontation with the elements. Indeed at no time in Bobrowski's poetry do we find a selective analytical description of an isolated object. The emphasis is always on the role played among other objects. Even when the original function has gone, a new significance is sought (see the forgotten dried-up well in *Der alte Brunnen*). The power of poetic interpretation, so often understood by Bobrowski as a trained process of careful listening, recreates the landscape (see *Language* (8), *Tree nymph* (9)). Yet it is nearly a 'lost language', for man, through neglect, forgetfulness, and a non-historical awareness of himself, has fragmented his environment and isolated himself from it. With this in mind *Always to be named* (7) is central to an understanding of Bobrowski's attitude.

There is a clear yet hesitant tension in *Always to be named* that has its place, not only in the contrasts between the first and the third, and between the second and the fourth verses, but also between the poet's isolation from and fascination with the landscape. Out of the poet's involvement in this tension the landscape is recreated, but he does not have the power to do more than name, sketch and colour its component parts. For those components have gone to sleep, lost contact with man, can be named but not directly spoken to. Colour and quiet movement reign in the first verse. The single nouns seem as if they had always been there, for each object is related to its own relevant element, and given its special frame. There is a variety of syntactical structure to express their individual relationship with the environment, and when it 'darkens over the woods', the night seems to come peacefully and naturally. Yet the poet sees this as a 'game', an idyllic description which he can no longer justify. For, as the third strophe shows, the landscape has gone to sleep. The objects are now made plural—the emblematic singular has but limited meaning in the everyday world. The idyllic first verse is shown to be no more than a lost arcadia. Sleep (used three times, never in the line with its appropriate noun, and most effectively filling a whole line by repetition to form a vacuous centre to the verse) has replaced a former state in which, as in the Romantics' vision of a Golden Age, direct speech between objects and with man was possible. Now 'in the darkness'—as a noun it has become a threatening, all-powerful feature of the landscape—the objects may 'still speak' (the German 'geht ihre Rede' suggests an uncertain, seeking, wandering voice). Not only are the objects out of contact with each other, but the poet has nobody to teach him how to describe that sleep. With no direct contact left with the landscape he knows his art is imperfect (in a Schillerian sense 'sentimental' rather than 'naiv'). A note of impatience appears : nearly all the earlier words of interrelationship are missing, the lines are shorter and frequently run together, the word-order and syntax are artificially reflective. Impatience turns in the final verse to desperation. The poet, lingering longingly over the idyllic first verse, is reduced before the last strophe to listening for a God, whose voice too cannot be heard. The poem moves from idyll to anxiety to estranged lament—the basic structure in Bobrowski's understanding of a tripartite time-scale in human consciousness.

6

CHARACTERISTICS OF PROSE STORIES

In an interview with Irma Reblitz in 1965—*Meinen Landsleuten erzählen, was sie nicht wissen*— Bobrowski commented on both his lyric and epic writings. He claimed to have no special reason for changing from composing mainly lyrics to mainly short prose pieces and a couple of novels. The forms of his writings seem to have followed his own appreciation of his abilities at each particular moment. There was no conscious attempt to be either a 'pure poet' or 'pure narrator', nor a programmatic desire to write so-called 'Mischformen'. As he himself points out, Bobrowski first tried to paint, then to compose, and then when he found he had friends who had far greater talent at doing both, 'I said to myself, well there's nothing left, so I shall start to write'. He also mentions a deeper reason: his desire to portray the landscape of Russia, which—because he had been held there as a prisoner of war—changed its aspect from the one he had known as a child. The war was no mere personal experience for Bobrowski, it also revealed to him the restrictions of traditional local German attitudes towards Eastern neighbours, attitudes that, as he continued to show, were based on ignorance and fear. Bobrowski's works seek to establish the falseness of such traditions and to inform new attitudes. Events and the scenery of the landscape form the cause for all his stories, but, as Bobrowski said in the Reblitz interview, 'History is not recapitulated in literature. But something new arises out of it'. The basic structure of his stories bears this out.

First comes a detailed building up of the setting with usually an emphatic concentration on the forces within it that form a link with the past. For instance, this may involve a comparison between the geographical setting of Königsberg and that of Rome with its seven hills (see *Der Mahner*), or the closely detailed description of a seascape painting with the professionalism of a trained observer of art linking the painting and the objects within it to nineteenth-century reports or travelogues (see *Looking at a picture* (22)), or merely the evocation of a sleepy litle forgotten town on a Sunday afternoon unchanging despite political and industrial progress (see *De homine publico tractatus* (27)). Then comes the intrusion into that setting of the character who

belongs to the past yet lingers on in the present—
usually in a quiet way limited to some special function in life yet with the fullness of human wisdom.
Thus we find the simple man from Lithuania standing beside the statue to the Kaiser, looking down on
the Nazis as they entered Königsberg and saying
'Keep God's commandments', and the man who has
built crosses on the cliff since his shipwreck and is
now gathering wood for a fire, and the post-office
official keeping all the rules but remaining human for
all that. Behind all of Bobrowski's stories lurks a
threat which is sometimes explicit, and often clear
condemnation of Nazi terror (see *Der Mahner*, the
poem *Report* (5)), and at least by implication *Mouse
banquet* (24); but often the threat lies in unthought-
ful inhumanity (*Letter from America* (23), *Epitaph
for Pinnau* (21)) or in officialdom (*Valéry or The
Beans* (26), *De homine publico tractatus* (27)). Central to many stories is the theme of forgetfulness seen
already in the poem *Elder blossom* (4); and also in
Letter from America (23), *Looking at a picture* (22).
It is not difficult to see in these stories the expression
of guilt aroused in so much post-1945 German literature by the theme of anti-Semitism, and it is clear
that on Bobrowski's avowal they have been generally
understood as such, especially by young people. But
one must question any quick dismissal of them as
forms of literary expiation for previous generations.

Expiation in the sense with which we may justly
understand this as part of Bobrowski's world is less a
single act or down payment to clear off a debt, than
the acceptance of a new and lasting attitude.
Bobrowski was too clear-sighted to believe in a
change of heart through a direct conversion of

human nature. His characters are for the most part resigned or become resigned to the at times inhuman parts of their nature (Kant in *Epitaph for Pinnau* (21), Klapschies in *Idylle für alte Männer*). That they are so is due to their acceptance of closeness to the past and its heritage. It is this closeness and the insistence on man's inability—to his own good—to throw off the past in a hurry that defines Bobrowski's purpose as a writer. It also determines his style and explains the unique sense of commitment and freedom that pervades his stories. His characters are committed within the time and place in which they are set (see especially *Boehlendorff* and *Levins Mühle*), yet they achieve a form of human detachment from it (see Moise Trumpeter in *Mouse banquet* (24), and the old woman in *Letter from America* (23)). Most of the stories are told in the present tense in order to involve the reader as much as possible.

The framework technique used in *Looking at a picture* (22) is an obvious example, in which we watch the writer take the picture, look at it, analyse it, and hang it on the wall. The story depicts the growing relationship between writer and picture inspired by the scene in the past portrayed in the picture. The masterly way in which the reader is led in and out of various narrative perspectives—in which, as it were, the story smoothly changes gear—constructs between writer and picture and between writer and reader an educative dialogue that leaves a most clear impression of the picture and its message without giving the feeling that the framework and narrative technique are unduly prominent. Thus the lingering yet subtly introduced paragraph on wooden houses to parallel the later paragraph describing the crosses and the fires. There is a sense of comfort evoked by houses and crosses as described, but there are cracks in the uncritical gaze, lessons of remembrance and warnings to be learnt from the events of the past.

In a similar manner, Bobrowski's stories all highlight an event, usually not one that alters the course of the characters' lives, but one that confirms or deepens their knowledge and understanding of life. The old woman in *Letter from America* (23) is no especially significant figure, nor is the particular event of the arrival of her son's letter of ultimate importance to mankind. Her burning of the photograph and letter is not in itself a symbolic act or an act of revenge, just a cancelling-out of one of her ways in life, one less link with her particularly set situation. The simplicity and preciseness of this story 'deheroises' the old woman, frees her gradually from all commitment and sentimentality.

Sometimes the event itself can be shown to have immediate consequence on the writer's art, as in *Valéry or The beans* (26). In this work Bobrowski attempts to describe Valéry's distance from the uniform of the Academy into which he has just been elected, and this he does through the image of the leather cloth drawn over a bean-plant. The image grows beyond its actual outward reality—in parallel perhaps to the organic growth of the beans and Valéry's own style—and develops a freedom of its own which leads Bobrowski away from depicting a portrait. Bobrowski suffers Lichtenberg's maxim : 'The metaphor is far cleverer than its creator'. Through his prose he bears witness to the martial growth of the beans under the helpful protection that lets in just enough light to help them grow. The contrast between the skeletal bean plant and the tender firmness of Valéry's skin, the natural qualities of the cloth and the gilt of the uniform, neatly bring out the deep irony of the photograph of Valéry's moment of 'glory' in the Academy robes, when, in fact, like the beans of the image, he was thrusting away beyond the tradition-bound premisses which gained him this recognition. Bobrowski has not only caught the essential moment or 'Motiv' when Valéry of all people is seen in uniform, but has worked back its effect on to the process of writing itself. The capital D of 'Die Bohnen' (or T of 'The beans') shows the actual separation of the two, brought together fruitfully by the artist's hand.

Bobrowski claimed that his stories all began without a plan and just as a game with light and shadows. The characters for the most part were not built from models in real life, but seemed to him to be readily believable. The conjunction of light and shadow is an essential structural device in both his poetry and his prose. It either points out man's subordinate position to the elements, or is a visual aid to encourage the reader to interpret the setting as a meeting-point of past and present or of conscious and semi-conscious. A consideration of his use of contrasts reveals the full force of counterpoint in Bobrowski's musical style. Even the extremely sudden shifts in narrative patterns are formally correct within the overall plan of his works.

His first story, *Es war eigentlich aus*, intermingles time perspectives and insistent memories with the result that the central character can free himself from a routine-bound existence. By narrating the events of

the past, he can reinterpret the present. The introduction of new unexpected characters points up the
lack of real association between individual characters,
places and events. Only one living thing in this story
is a confident tie between the three factors : namely,
the black dog by the station door. Even the dog,
ironically enough, is recognised as a different breed
than beforehand. Attachment to a landscape because
of a past event within it is shown up as a false reality.
The role of the unfamiliar or unexpected has therefore a liberating force in Bobrowski's works of
undoubted significance.

The eighteenth-century style of *Epitaph for Pinnau*
(21), with its contrast between the formal mathematic-
ally exact protocol of Kant's circle and the deafness
and inhumanity towards Pinnau, makes Pinnau's sui-
cide a challenge to the values of this closed-in social
group. Kant's epitaph to Pinnau is that he died
'Cavalirement', a formal Frenchified word that in
this context discloses an indictment on the whole setting in which it is uttered. It is perhaps an indication
of bad conscience, or a quick sign of deference in a
situation where the group as a social destroyer is even
reflected in the treeless exterior of Kant's house. The
banal details of the gathering and the uncultured
behaviour of the members of the circle seem totally
irrelevant and inhuman when seen side by side with
the details of Pinnau's death. The artificially constructed, ill-balanced behaviour of Kant's circle as
portrayed here sacrifices individual freedom of
expression. The closed circle can only be shown up
for what it is in human terms through local tragedy,
or an unexpected act. This is the sharpest and most
effective attack Bobrowski made on the inhumanity

of pure reason to the exclusion of all that is individual, illogical and maybe second-rate.

Perhaps the most marked feature of Bobrowski's stories is the variety in their style. In contrast with the precise, ordered crispness of style in such works as *Epitaph for Pinnau* (21), or *D.B.H.*, the phantasy *Von nachgelassenen Poesien* seems little more than a delightful whimsy. It starts with the two central verses of a poem left unfinished when a poet dies. These verses are themselves the product of his musing and conversations in his grave. The search for a beginning and end to the poem allows the narrator to indulge in a description of the personal feelings, social attitudes and enjoyments of the poet. The reader is kept at a respectful distance and is never allowed to construct any logical interpretation to the phantasies described. The development towards the simple final verse in the manner of the Baroque poet Simon Dach, a graveyard chorale, is compact and fleeting. In fact the final paragraph, with no main clause verb, condenses the process of the creation of posthumous poetry into a style that is already half way to becoming poetry itself :

Always then before you lie back. No screaming. Katharina, a white face. Doves' wings across a broken wall and down. Where it is dark. Who would have to scream. The electoral prince, prince, prince. The Adersbach, Adersbach, Adersbach. Posthumous poetry. Who would have to scream. Posthumous poetry. No-one. That bit about the Alkgebirge, Dach has that as well.

Through this story we are forced to realise that the conditions of poetry, its setting and its genesis, can be alarmingly different from the style into which the poetry is set. Place, character and event are separated out. The contrast between the harshness of human life and death with the constructed serenity of poetic praise and lament is resolved in a playful yet by no means escapist story.

This same Baroque insistence on facing up to reality, yet playfully accepting and patterning away its harshest features in balancing rhythms, can be seen in the shattering contrast in length of *The first two sentences for a book on Germany* (25). The movement and expression of different styles in the first sentence, so real in its painstaking syntax of explaining away and in its vague inhuman vocabulary, is utterly exploded by the sober, abstracted yet pointed precision of the short second sentence.

The principle of contrast and meticulous use of style are used most effectively in *Idylle für alte Männer*. Klapschies' vice is gluttony, and Bobrowski does not need to describe this in great detail, merely in the simple visionary temptation and setting of an old man's vision :

And now [5 a.m.!] Klapschies is hungry. That is a feeling. One could describe it directly : just as it rises up in you. But the little woman's not there. Gone among the berries. Bilberries. Towards evening a nice bowl full, covered in milk and sugar.

Dependent on his wife for food, he is driven out of the house by hunger, and a description of the local roads follows almost as if on a menu. Musing on this causes Klapschies to forget his work of looking after

49

the horses. And in *Volkslied* style the idyllic fascination with the landscape is broken: 'Was meinst du, wie die Pferde gehen, wenn der Hafer lockt!' Klapschies remembers a local scandal about the birth and upbringing of the man he goes to visit, and he recalls this in a record-card style. Everything is cut down to a minimum, the whole background of Parbandt is explained in a few words. At the same time the restricted interests of village-life, its parochialism and its interest in other people's misfortunes, the rather hushed awe and secretive delight in the shockingly immoral: all are made into a story, narrative becomes part of Klapschies' staple diet. Ridicule at tradition, national pride and the role of the church is managed through the story of the great round oak tables cut out of a huge tree felled some years back— 'Such German oaks, healthy and lasting like the plague! The priest had preached about it, the community should take this marvel of fidelity and endurance as an example ['Treue und Beständigkeit' with obvious reference to the *O Tannenbaum* Christmas carol], saw down a spiritual slice from the tree, now that each had his portion and the tree had gone'. As soon as hunger is stilled, more stories are told. Parbandt, Klapschies' friend, is sharply criticised by his wife for preparing his own grave: 'Die first, the rest will be arranged later'. Proverbial style sets in when Klapschies returns home: 'An old man is like a shadow, once he springs over the fence, he is on the other side'. Gradually he is portrayed as the old man: getting tired, his concentration lapses, his mind drifts, and the style becomes looser. Words are repeated both to show the monotony and as points of reference in the rambling idyll that is really a decline.

The spirit of truth—a favourite subject of the priest's prayers—can only come from the priest to Klapschies in a glass of schnaps. Gradually Bobrowski develops the contrast of idyllic atmosphere and irrevocable waiting on death. Klapschies' circle is complete in his rounds of hunger and thirst, and even his dignity is shown to be meaningless at such a stage in life. Yet in the implied incompletion and emptiness of his existence there reigns a certain order. The old man, for all his weaknesses, emerges as a triumphant example of the human spirit. Bobrowski reinstates the quality of his life by pointing out its limits and by insisting on Klapschies' independence, which remains vigorous and defiant to the end.

7

NOVELS

Vigour and defiance are indeed the characteristic responses to life of the central figure in Bobrowski's first and best-known novel *Levins Mühle*. Not surprisingly when we know Bobrowski's gentle humanity, the Grandfather is neither revered nor utterly condemned in this book. Indeed it is hard to find any total condemnation or unmitigated praise for any of Bobrowski's characters—they are all too human and too sharply observed for simple categorisation in grades of good or evil. The whole substructure of *Levins Mühle* is a declared warning on the part of the narrator that reality as he tries to describe it is necessarily incomplete and should not be interpreted superficially. The sub-title *Vierunddreißig Sätze über meinen Großvater* distances the narrator from his subject, never allowing the reader to assume that Bobrowski is firmly on the side of his Grandfather's character. It also invites the reader to judge the issues and events of the novel detachedly and separately from historical connotations, religious views, narrative traditions or even legal evidence. The search for, definition of and expansion into chapters of the thirty-four relevant sentences keep the reader critically awake and open-minded, and also serve to give the story some form of pattern, a unity which the events themselves do not naturally have, and which it would seem we are not encouraged to make up for them. The narrator's repeated discussions of the progress of his story do away with the formation of a literary reality built up by the reader and encouraged by the author. Imagination is held firmly in its place, either by its deliberate and clear siting in particular characters' minds—often when they are half drunk for example—or in the device of the Grandfather's 'Geistererscheinungen': vivid ghostly visions experienced when he is unconscious. These in particular make the reader aware of underlying links between the ethics and general behaviour of individuals and society in previous generations back to the sixteenth and seventeenth centuries, with the particular codes of local and state behaviour in 1874 around the lower reaches and tributaries of the River Vistula, and with the more modern attitudes of the narrator himself. Judgement on the characters, whether legal, moral, religious or generally human, has to take this broadening view of time into account. At no moment can the reader approach the work simply from the point of view of any particular century.

Because of this, the episodic nature of the book threatens to become exemplary. The legal entanglements of the Grandfather's and Levin's case neither escalate into never-ending action and counter-action, nor does it become a cause célèbre. This is partly due to the detached wisdom of a district judge, but also to a certain inborn resilience to misfortune in most of the main characters. Bobrowski's narrative style, especially in his two novels, is largely conversational. The formal literary canon of third person framework description or first person inner monologue gives way to a forever shifting dialogue between the characters themselves, characters and author, author and reader. By this Bobrowski appears to have immersed himself in the lives of his characters, the atmosphere of his stories' landscapes. The thirty-four sentences are not in themselves of equal significance, nor are the situations out of which they arise. Yet, such is the directness and finality of their wisdom in context that they force the author to acknowledge their aptness as phrases which sum up and interpret separate features within the overall mosaic of the story. Reality is shown as episodic and subject to the social, cultural and psychological limitations of the characters involved. Its meaning and resultant motivation for the characters grow out of the power of telling phrases that are the comments reached by the characters after involvement in preceding events. This process is particularly clear, for example, with the evocation of anger and pride by the singing of patriotic songs to past heroes of the peasants' revolt of 1863. Bobrowski finds that the numbered and unnumbered sentences must have two important qualities in order to be promoted from subordinate to main sentences—'striking brevity, and, above all, feeling'. However insignificant sentences may look in themselves, they are the culmination and distillation of complex feelings aroused by episode and encounter. The episodic in the book attains significance through a process of formulation by individual character. Language once again is the creative power that develops subjective experience into significant truth.

The actual story concerns the legal proceedings and local relationships following on the apparently wilful destruction of a mill. Grandfather Johann, whose prices as the owner of a mill with Polish employees are undercut in a smaller self-run mill by a newcomer the Jew Levin, sees himself as the leading villager. He is German, a Baptist and loyal to his Kaiser. Levin, although poor, represents a financial and consequently social, anti-patriotic and above all psychological threat to Johann. The motivation is so strong, that although no-one saw him do it, Johann is generally recognised as the destroyer of Levin's mill. Levin seeks justice through the German, Christian legal system. To defend his position Grandfather forms the 'Malkener Union' involving an apparently oecumenical body of support including the local priests, the policeman and legal officials. This threat of immigrant interference with the local German economic and social system can neither be tolerated, nor can it be allowed to undermine German self-esteem as the local governing class. Only Kaplan Rogalla stands out against such a selective form of brotherly love, and even he is prevented from active support of the minority.

The actual series of delayed legal sessions, of intrigues, imprisonment of witnesses, and the burning

down of another building is in itself complex enough
to suggest the playing out of determined self-interests,
the expression of a calculated, self-protective system.
But alongside this harshness and inhumanity,
Bobrowski portrays a whole spectrum of local everyday life; dictated by the demands of the landscape he
uses terms of endearing and at times whimsical
delight. There are lyrical passages in this novel—such
as the love scene in the rain, the simple journey by
road to Malken, or the burial scene—that stand out
because they would have happened regardless of any
of the characters' involvement in the Johann-Levin
conflict. They are timeless and therefore seem to have
an air of formality about them quite different from
the forced and somewhat ridiculous playing to rule of
the legal system. Officialdom and humanity are thus
shown to be far removed from each other. Despite
the complex structure and frequent intrusion of the
narrator into the story, the directness, colloquialisms,
simplicity and forthright knowledge of good and evil
from a subjective standpoint on the part of the main
characters make this a delightful book to read and a
major achievement as a novel of village life.

Episode and encounter are the basis of Bobrowski's
second novel *Litauische Claviere*. This suffers in direct comparison with *Levins Mühle*, for much of its
artistic intention and local allusion overwhelms the
clear and full characterisation that is such an attractive feature of *Levins Mühle*. The characters in
Litauische Claviere, their actions and their lives, are
all too obviously intentionally seen through the focus
of the story's quest. They are directly connected with
the author, not so much like puppets on a string, but
as carefully chosen actors in a special situation. None

of them have enough vigour and defiance to bring about a radical change of direction in the story—in contrast to the Grandfather in *Levins Mühle*—but all are conditioned by their local and national heritage. It would perhaps be false to expect otherwise in a description of two days : Saturday 23 June 1936 and the following Sunday, a Sunday of traditional folk festivals celebrated in the villages differently by Germans and Lithuanians. The intrusion of Professor Voigt, a member of the German-Lithuanian Society, a 'Reichsdeutscher' actively seeking to improve relations between the two local communities, and of the orchestral conductor Gawehn into these festivals on the search for material to help their opera on the Lithuanian poet Donelaitis, is purely humanitarian. The problem is whether such an approach is relevant to the local political situation.

The idea for writing such an opera stemmed from the outstanding character of Christian Donelaitis himself, the first great Lithuanian poet born in 1714 in a local village and educated in the school where Bobrowski himself went as a child. Donelaitis was renowned locally as a preacher in both German and Lithuanian, as a highly skilled gardener, a maker of optical glasses, barometers, thermometers and pianos, also as a poet, composer and pianist. In particular it is interesting to note that he made extensive use of classical hexameters in his poetry—a form particularly suited it seems to the Lithuanian language—before Klopstock. Bobrowski was fascinated by this feature of Donelaitis, and also by Hamann's comments in *Christliche Bekenntnisse und Zeugnisse* on the marked similarity of Lithuanian working songs with the metre of classical Greek poets. He marked off the following comment for instance in his edition of Hamann : 'If a poet should emerge from them, it would be natural that all his lines should be cut to the pattern of this metre'. This persistence of classical resemblance through the local poet, accepted as a unifying and humane influence by both local peoples, was likely to attract Bobrowski's interest on personal grounds, but also at a time when the whole problem of the relevance of culture in a divided community was sharply present to him.

In Bobrowski's novel there is a search for form to express the totality of a divided community. That form has to take into account the reasons for the division, historical, psychological, geographical, etc., and weld them together into a complete statement of the situation. The transference of local event, episode and encounter into part of a mosaic by the writer, or, as we see here, by characters who are musicians, desubjectivises individual attachment to that event. The projected opera and Bobrowski's novel produce through their form a total perspective that is impossible for any of the characters within the situation's network of commitments.

Bobrowski chose a moment in local history that brought to a head the tension between the local communities. The annual fête of the *Vaterländischen Frauenvereins Luisenbund* took place at the same moment as the Lithuanian celebrations in honour of Vytautas. (The local branch of the women's association would in fact be celebrating the historical meeting of the Prussian Queen Louise with the Emperor Napoleon in a belated manifestation of 'Hurrah-Patriotismus' at which Bobrowski clearly found it difficult to suppress a certain smile. The great King

Vytautas was celebrated as a legendary figure by those who still supported the cause of a Greater-Lithuania.)

By misfortune a brawl between supporters of the different parties takes place and one person is killed. In itself this background appears trivial, and perhaps all too typical. But the dating of the encounter in 1936 adds a further dimension. Since 1933, a local Nazi leader under the guise of the fascist Memel Party had been installed to further Hitler's interests in a revision of the border against the local Lithuanian nationalist government. Hitler refused a pact of non-aggression with Lithuania in 1936, and the Memel Party won more and more support at local elections. 1936 became a year of calm before the storm, a year of mounting tension behind the scenes, a year of false reliance on traditional custom and celebration in the face of a new order which was clearly bound to take over in the near future.

Bobrowski's novel includes a strain of underlying tension that is played out, as it were, on the different instruments of landscape : description, social groupings, individual memories, limitations of personal perspectives, etc. It is all the more effective because this is set against the major theme of idyllic illusion and hope. Yet neither of these attitudes is real enough, central enough for Bobrowski. In a masterly chapter the device of an observation tower is used for climbing out above the restricted vision of the local village group and of the present historical moment. From the top an overall view of the landscape is gained, from the top the present moment in time is reduced in significance. Just as the local subjective commitments are avoided, so too are the ties with the immediate present. The past and to a certain extent the future are allowed to ridicule any fervent attitudes or fears. Because life has continued despite everything through generations of oppression and readjustment, hope is found and expressed through a reintegration of the individual with a limited task. Donelaitis' pianos are remade. The voice of Donelaitis continues as the only lasting voice beyond conquest and suppression. Bobrowski's final novel, completed only a few weeks before his death, is a search for and rediscovery of an apparently dying language.

8

CONCLUSION

The works of Johannes Bobrowski are marked by their refusal to accept surface values as the true human expression of life. They were written not out of fear, but with a sober-minded optimism in the good sense and capacity for survival of the human race. They assume certain basic features about man, and they speak directly to those who share such beliefs: equally of man in the face of threat and danger, love of peace, the need for meaningful activity, a dislike of regimentation of the mind or body, a dislike, too, of artificiality and all its trappings (for example, uniform), and love of colour and order in the landscape. They call for patience, careful listening, and confidence in self-expression. As works of art, they are outstanding for their development of a compact yet varied style; for their penetrating appraisal of essential aesthetic qualities; their immediate appeal as they reach out to the reader through rhythm or colloquialism or active apostrophe; their rich allusive quality to traditional local historical and folklore culture; their unobtrusive use of classical education and knowledge; and, above all, for their reticent—and at times humorous—refusal to parade as great works of art. If Bobrowski's works can be understood as a lament to man's estrangement, then it is a lament without pathos. For above all, Bobrowski was a craftsman, and literature for him became the craft of life.

Bobrowski was clearly a most individual writer. All too easily dismissed as an escapist who took refuge from a hostile environment in his art, his life and works can also be raised wrongly as an ideal way of life, as an easy way out, or as a contemplative monastic withdrawal. Several features counteract such a legend. First of all, Bobrowski himself was the true craftsman in that he was primarily concerned with the quality of the work performed rather than in its revelation of the artist. His own person was of little consequence as a central point to his art. There is no self-aggrandisement, no self-seeking, no demand for self-satisfaction in his poetry.

Instead, Bobrowski recognised his place and turned from contemplation of his own situation to a conscious deliberate expression of the dangers and possibilities of man's future. Despite his conviction that man has taken the wrong road in demanding more and more technical progress, Bobrowski looked forward all the time to a better, fearless future. He believed that the variety of the human spirit had saved it from destruction in the past. From this came a belief in self-expression not as a way to conquest and superiority over others, but as a continual process of adjustment with natural laws. His works are part of his adjustment and are therefore personal rather than didactic. In fact they are Bobrowski's attempt to define his relationship with the time and place in which he found himself, not a way out of time. They attempt a total vision of a limited perspective in that he reveals his awareness of previous events influencing current behaviour.

His understanding of the richness of language and of its confusion through the deposit of allusion on every single word did not prevent him from catching sight of 'dead' language and reinstating it in simple forms in his poetry (see *Language* (8)). His interest in other languages and literatures, in history and local geography, in mythology and local custom, suggests a search for exemplary situations or characters in which the individual comes to terms with his environment and does something to restore it out of the scars of the past. His works all present a challenge to the characters set in them. They demand gestures of renewed commitment, sometimes of memory, sometimes of hope. Bobrowski's art was to isolate, define and emphasise challenge and commitment. In doing so he justified rather than idealised his own existence. In keeping close to this essentially primitive aim he produced works which seem limited in purpose but had great variety of technical device. The compactness and precision of their form and allusion can only stem from a thorough knowledge of their setting. We may sum them up as the edited dialogues of a landscape gardener, who, having inherited a wilderness, is seeking to reconstruct some of the lost order to leave for the future.

TRANSLATIONS

(1) *Invocation*

Wilna, oak tree
you—
my birch,
Novgorod—
once in the woods flew up
the cry of my springtimes, my days'
tread rang out across the flood.

Ah, the bright gleam,
the summer stars, all are given away,
and down by the fire
squats the teller of tales,
those young ones who listened nightlong
away have gone.

Lonely he will sing :
across the steppes
roam the wolves, the huntsman
found a yellowing stone,
it flared up in the moonshine.

Holiness swims,
a fish,
through the old valleys, the wooded
valleys still, the voice of
fathers still peals out :

65

Give welcome to strangers.
You shall be a stranger. Soon.

(2) *Pruzzian elegy*

To sing you
one song,
bright with an angry love—
yet dark, bitter with
lament, wet like the meadow—
weeds, as on coastfall the
bare pines, moaning
beneath the wan wind of dawn,
burning before evening—

your never sung-to
decline, which struck us once
in the blood, when our days
all hung full of child's play
wide open to dreams—

then in the woods of our homeland
above the foam-tossed
green of the sea, where with the smoke
of sacrificial groves
we shuddered, before stones,
by long sunken gravemounds,
grass-grown ramparts, under the linden
bent down lightly with age—

how rumour hung in its branches!
So in the old crones' songs
sounds yet,
now hard to make out,

a call from before time—
how there we heard then
rotting the echo, lingering
dimly-blanched pall!
So there remains
from deep bells, the broken ones,
just a thin tinkling—

People
of the black woods,
of heavily thrusting rivers,
of bare haffs, and of the sea!
People
of nocturnal hunts,
of herds and the bright summer-fields!
People
of Perkun and Pikoll,
of the garlanded corn-god Patrimpe!
People
like none else, of full joy!
like none else, none else, of death!

People
of the smouldering groves,
of the burning huts, of trampled down
green corn, of blood-reddened rivers—
People
sacrificed to the scorching
thunderbolt; your cries all shrouded in
cloud-banks of flame—
People
before the unknown god's
mother plunging in throat-rasping
dance—

how before her brazen
armed might she paces, rising up
over the wood! how the Son's
gallows follows her trace!—

Names speak of you still,
you stamped-down people, hillsides,
rivers, gleam rarely showing,
stones too and roads—
songs in the evening and legends,
the rustle of lizards still names you
and like water in the marsh
now a song its plaint made
poor—
poor like the fisherman's catch,
that eternal white-haired one,
on the haff, when the sun
goes down on the sea.

(3) *Lake Ilmen 1941*

Wilderness. Against the wind.
Numb. The river sunk
into the sand.
Charred the branches:
the village before the clearing. And then
we saw the lake—

—Days of the lake. Of light.
In the rough track, in the grass
out there the tower,
white, gone from his stone like the
dead. The shattered roof
with its cawing crows.

—Nights of the lake. The wood
towards the marshes
drops down. The old wolf
fat from the burnt-out site
startled by a phantom shade.
—Years of the lake. The brazen
flood. The rising darkness
of the waters. Down from the sky
one day
will strike down the storming birds.

Did you see the sail? Fire
stood in the distance. The wolf
paced into the clearing.
Listens for the bells of winter.
Howls for the enormous
cloud of snow.

(4) *Elder blossom*

There comes
Babel, Isaak.
He says : In the pogrom,
and I a child,
my pigeon's head,
they tore it off.

Houses in the wooden streets,
with fences, elder over them.
Scrubbed white the threshold,
little stairs going down—
But then, remember,
the bloodstain.

Holunderblüte (Elder blossom)

People, you declaim : Forget—
for youngsters are coming
their laughter like bushes of elder.
People, the elder may
well die
of your forgetfulness.

(5) *Report*

Bajla Gelblung
escaped in Warsaw
from a transport from the ghetto,
the girl
took to the woods,
armed, was picked up,
a partisan
in Brest-Litovsk,
wore a military coat (Polish),
was interrogated by German
officers, there is
a photo, the officers are young
men, immaculate uniforms,
immaculate faces,
their bearing
is unexceptionable.

(6) *Dead language*

He who beats with his wings
outside, who brushes the door,
that is your brother, you hear him.
Laurio he says, water,
a bow's bend, colourless, deep.

Bericht (Report)

He came down here with the stream,
round mussel and snail came
drifting, a fan-like growth
on the sand and was green.

Warne he says and *wittan,*
the crow it has no tree,
I have the power to kiss you,
I dwell in your listening ear.

Tell him you don't
wish to hear him—
he comes, an otter, he comes
swarming like hornets, he cries,
a cricket, he grows with the marsh
under your house, in the wells
he whispers, *smordis* you gather,
your black alder will wither,
tomorrow it dies at the fence.

(7) *Always to be named*

Always to be named :
the tree, the bird in flight,
the reddish rock where the stream
slips, green, and the fish
in the white mist, when it darkens
over the woods.

To sketch and colour is but
a game I fear
that might not end
as it should.

73

And who will teach me
what I forgot : the stones'
sleep, the sleep
of the birds in flight, the trees'
sleep, in the darkness
do they still speak—?

If a God was but there
and incarnate,
and could call to me, then I
would walk around, I would
linger a while.

(8) *Language*

The tree
greater than the night
with the breath of the valley-lakes
with the whispering over
the stillness

The pebbles
under one's foot
the glittering veins hid
long in the dust
for ever

Language
overworked
with one's tired mouth
on the endless way
to a neighbour's house.

(9) *Tree nymph*

> Birch, cool
> with the sap, tree, breath
> in my hands, tensed
> the bark, a brittle glass,
> yet to sense deeper
> stirring, the reaching upwards
> from bole,
> and out to the furthest twigs.
>
> Let
> down to the neck
> let fall your hair, I hear
> in my hands, I hear a moving,
> hear mounting the current,
> a rising flood,
> the torrent
> sing in my ear.

(10) *Kalmus*

> With rain-set sails around
> flies a-howling
> the water-wind.
> A blue dove
> has spread its wings
> over the wood.
> Gay in the shattered iron
> of the fern
> goes the light
> with the head of a pheasant.
>
> Breath,

I send you forth,
find you a roof,
go in through a window, in the white
mirror catch sight of you,
turn you quietly,
a green sword.

(11) *Trip in the cart*

O beautiful moon of Mariampol! On your
straw-like rim my little town,
behind the stalls
up he comes,
heavy, and hangs a little
downwards. Thus goes the
horse dealer, he buys
for his mother a fringed shawl.

At nightfall
late
they both sang. We crossed
over the river homewards
on the ferry, with call and answer
our chatter flowed light as the
water—and we heard him so long
across the town
up there in the towers, heard
the Jewish moon. He is
like in the garden's corner the little
plant of weeping and kisses,
rue, our girls
they break it off.

Joneleit, come, do not lose

Wagenfahrt (Trip in the cart)

your shawl. The old ones are sleeping.
Sung through once more
is a night.

(12) *Russian songs*

Maryna
down from a tower
across the landscape of rocks
singing, three rivers
beneath at her feet, but
night and the wind's
shadows in flight.

You my fairest,
my tree,
high in the branches
with brow bared
to the moon
I sleep, nestled
into my wings.

I sleep—
you give me a grain of salt
scooped from an untravelled
sea, I give you
a drop of rain
from the land
of no weeping.

(13) *Icon*

Towers, arched, fenced in
with crosses, red. Dark
breathes the sky, Joann

Russische Lieder (Russian songs)

stands on the hill, the town
against the river. He watches
the sea come in with planks,
oars, scaling
fish, the wood
casts itself down into the sand.
Into the wind
strides the prince, brandishing
torches in both hands, he strews
silent fires
over the steppes.

(14) *In the stream*

With the rafts downwards
in the lighter grey of the other
bank, to a
gleam, which withdraws, to the grey
of slanting surfaces, from mirrors
we were shot at by light.

There lay the Baptist's head
on its mutilated eyebrow
into its torn-through hair
a hand clawed in fast with bluish
loose-fitting nails.

When I loved you, disturbed was
your heart, a meal on the beating
fire, the mouth, which then opened,
wide open, the stream
was a rain and flew
with the herons, leaves
fell and filled up its bed.

We stooped over stunned
fish, decked out in scales
trod the cricket's song
across the sand, from the bowers
on the bank, we had come
just to sleep. No-one
prowled round our camp. No-one
put out the mirrors. No-one
will wake us
in our good time.

(15) *The Don*

High, the villages
of fire. Over the rock
the banks plunge down. But
the river caught, it breathed
ice, stillness darkly
followed it on.

White was the river. The higher
bank dark. The horses
climbed up the slope. Once
the banks opposite
fled away, we saw,
behind the fields, far,
under the early moon, walls
against the sky.

There
sings the Div
in the tower,
he cries to the cloud, the bird
all of ill-omen, he calls

81

across the rocky banks,
commands the plains to hear.
Hills, open up, he says,
stand forth in your armour,
o dead ones, put on your helmet.

(16) *Reawakening*

The
land
empty,
through spread-out cloths
the other greens up, laid out
beneath, that once before
was
a misgiving. It comes
from the plague time, white
with bones, ribs, vertebrae,
radii, with the lime.

Count
the grasses
and count
filaments of rain water,
and light, leaflets too
count, and register
your paces, spoors of the hunted,
and voices, enliven
with words
the blood in the trees and
the lungs, beat
rust down from walls
and steps,
on your hands

it lingers, there may it be
nourished
with your nails.

It is not the time to ask it.
It is the time for the water
on plant stems, for the renewed
sprouting of leaves, and may their green
open up eyes.

(This poem was written for Paul Celan)

(17) *Barlach in Güstrow*

Stones,
the multiple arch
locked
by the iron veins
of the door. Threshold
with spare grass
and plantain in the earth.
I stand,
stick drawn towards me.

That's nothing :
going around, other ways.
Who that was,
he who set earthen birds
on a closed-in sward,
I have forgotten.
He sat on the meadow. With wisps of smoke
facelessly
this day goes by.

Smoke.
There the arch.
Light streams down from the roofs.
The pebble beneath the shoe,
at evening, the pebble,
at evening
the pebble
is caught.

(18) *Ode to Thomas Chatterton*

Mary Redcliffe, red, a mountain range beneath
your towers, beneath the rambling cornices
and the walls, steep jig-sawed cut of the arches,
trickling with shadows . . .

here the child grew up with his speech alone as
with his hands, helpless; who wandered often
by night: stood on the hanging parapet, looked
out blind on the town

asleep under the moon, where a gravedigger
    worked
sighing in the graveyard plot—, called back
times passed away with worn-out names.
Ah, she would never

awaken, so he went, to find life in the voices
of friends, in the soft nestling brows
of his girls, so in the narrow coffins
he laid their heads down.

Would no longer come, when he called it, the
    past.

But only his doubt, solitary echo, flew
dustily creaking with him the stair, soft as an
    owl
for him the tower clock struck.

Just to speak out : that he died away so,
his songs full of dusk—Daily we pull forth
something unthinkable, yet whatever
we had against time,

always some meaning was there, just the
    slightest,
moving now him and now him : then perhaps
    is a
tree, in full green, a twig-shooting, myriad
rustling roofwork of leaves;

a shadow lurks underneath—, yet shading not
    the
slender trace of despair : travelled thus far
pale lightning-flash, where hardly a cloud stood,
ruffled into the blue,

over that town, which with its fears went on,
Bristol, as the boy sung, out there
on the Avon, where still the meadow-dew
for ever still knew him.

O but the owl-wings of childhood over
his paces, as in strange streets by
bridges he found under the windswept roofs
a passing embrace

and death too; it came pale as poured tea,

stood by the table, slipping into the shaking
    leaves,
on the writing its bony finger, 'Rowley'
he read, 'Aella'.

(19) *Village music*

Final boat in which I fare
hat no more upon my hair
in four oak-boards joined and white
rue-sprigs in the hand held tight
walking round my friends feel great
      one now blows upon the trumpet
      one now blows upon the trombone
boat don't sink beneath such weight
hear the others talking grand :
'this one built upon the sand'

Beside the well there calls the crow
from the branchless pole : 'O woe'
from the tree all bare and trim :
'take the parting gift from him
take those twigs of rue away'
      but there blares out loud the trumpet
      but there blares out loud the trombone
no-one's snatched my rue away
all just say : 'from time to go
'tis not far for him you know'

Now I know too and I fare
hat no more upon my hair
moonlight round my beard and brow
lived out no more fooling now
hark once more from down below

for again there sounds the trumpet
for again there sounds the trombone
and from far off calls the crow
I am where I am : in sand
with the rue held in my hand.

(20) *The word man*

The word man, alphabetically
placed where it belongs
in the Concise Oxford
between mammy and manacle.

The town
old and new,
nice and busy, with trees
too
and vehicles, here

I hear the word, its vocable
I hear frequently here, I can
count up from whom, I can
make a start with that.

Where love is not there,
don't say that word.

(21) *Epitaph for Pinnau*

In front of Kant's house there stands no tree. Is
the street really so narrow? How is it that you never
come past the two-storied bare cote without brushing
the front wall with sleeve and shoulder? And taking

away again some of the bright plaster? One day—
that we can safely say already—the wall-tiles which
today are still covered will be visible : a light red for
which the colour green will then be lacking, for in
front of Kant's house there stands no tree. Behind the
house and round one of the gables lies a little garden.
That is too little. But stuck to the house, there, there
is a coop for hens. So at least we have these strangely
arguing bird voices, which converse or do not—you
never know, you listen, and when the coppersmith
down on the Schloßberg is hammering away a little
and the clock of the castle tower tinkles down the
wrong hour, or the right one, you only miss the clat-
ter of hurriedly taken-up sticks—sticks with sheet-iron
tips and silver heads, black or dark brown sticks—for
everything to be there : a concentus sufficient to describe the English town of London and how it lies on
the River Thames, or a conflagration in Stockholm,
which out of deference stops short of Swedenborg's
house.

But now the impatient sticks approach and become
too loud. The sticks are a plague for him who wanted
to listen to the concentus. 'Gobble up nicely, my little
hens,' says the old woman and goes back into the
kitchen. There stands Kant in his little brown frockcoat shaking pepper out of a little yellow box on to
the nice food. And the sticks have reached the front
door. Set themselves down each with a little clink on
the stone slab in front of the threshold, each a
destination at the end of a quick approach—from the
Junkergarten, from the Steindamm, from the Lizent-
graben. Punctuality, gentlemen.

Up then with the sticks now and into the house.
Strong Scheffner calls out loud for all to hear : 'And

a very good day to you,' and Lampe the servant says: 'Thank you, my Lord Councillor of War,' and takes his cloak from him. And Professor Schulz pushes his way in, hangs his coat over Lampe's shoulder and plants his hat on him, and Lampe says astonished: 'But yes, my Head Court Chaplain, yes.' I should have taken his first, he realises, while elegant Motherby is ready stabbing his little stick impatiently into the small of his back, only gently of course. 'We, you know, are invited, man,' and throws the coat over the bannister, where, by the way, Court Bookseller Kanter's things are already lying. The latter turns round in the hall, and Borowski and Wasianski too, one long and thin, the other short and plump, Scheffner, the fattest in the middle, Schultz getting more and more squat down below, shapes of cylindrical wooden dolls, lozenges, skittle pins, with tailor's model Motherby gracefully between. So then up the stairs. Kanter is already standing there in the open doorway, has quickly cast an eye over the table—everything in place—and so looks down reassured over the stairs, where he discovers Hamann's frockcoat tails in the kitchen door, and now the tails too have vanished, the door is closed, and Lampe is threading his way through the gentlemen on the stairs and saying, once he has reached the top, composed and rigidly: 'His Professorship is in t' kitchen, but come there all the same.' And down below the door opens again and the old woman, the cook, calls up: 'Yes, come at once, and you Mr. Lampe, come on down.'

So Lampe steps down. The gentlemen all at the same moment draw out their splendid chronometers; it is, you see, striking twelve from the castle tower, and as all is silent again, you cannot only hear the strokes of the clock, but between them the rattling and panting of the clock's mechanism.

Down in the kitchen where it is all a bit steamy, stand Kant and Hamann. 'Pinnau, you said?'

'But I know them too, good family,' says the cook.

'No, we mean the son,' says Kant.

'Pretty boy with black 'air,' says the woman.

'Bookkeeper Pinnau,' says Hamann, 'he's dead, this morning, I hear a shot in the next room and run there, and Pinnau is lying shot in the face and is already dead.'

'What was wrong with Pinnau,' asks Kant, 'wasn't he taking his degree at the licentiate?'

'He thought out ...'—Hamann puts his hat on again, which he has been passing from one hand to the other, changing all the time with stick and cloak. 'He wrote pieces of poetry . . . he wanted something out of the question,' he says. And Kant replies quickly and tonelessly : 'You too, then?'

Upstairs the gentlemen are walking about on the white boards, to the window, into the room again, round the table. Where is the lord of the house then? And now Lampe comes with the tureen and behind him, small and lightly, just as if the stairs had carried him up, Kant, and close to him—morning coat too long, coat over his arm, hat on his head, like a raven with feathers all dishevelled through getting into a current of wind, and with a black stick—Customs Overseer Hamann.

'He did not come here to listen,' says Kant, 'did he at all?'

With this he steps into the room a little confused

because he hears Hamann behind him answer: 'Yes, at my place.'

Schulz looks meaningfully at Borowski the Neuross-garten priest, and both shake their heads, and that means: Hamann? He is indeed neither Licentiate nor Master, but the head-shaking fits well with the dance of the skittle-pins and lozenges, cylindrical wooden dolls and I don't know what else, that now starts up again.

Kanter with outstretched arms, which he brings together behind his back as if he wanted to encompass the air behind him, as it were the world, at least the town, or rather three towns, the status of which they had only recently gained, embrace together with them their seven hills, bring them to the great one, to the wise one—why, what am I saying: to the wisdom of the world itself. With this three, four little paces. And Scheffner! A quick eager bow: Thus it is, when you tear yourself the wreath of honour of an amorous poet from his noble brow, out of admiration. Thus it looks! And Schultz, who, as mathematician, knows best what the illustrious colleague signifies: a star. Of the first magnitude of course. And the others circle around it and make elliptical paths towards it, once again a little dance, charmingly, for the twelve clock strokes are past, and the town pipers down from the tower are blowing their midday chorale across the roofs and into the houses as if they had to cool the soup of rich and poor alike.

Kant keeps his most friendly short words of greeting ready, turns round a little at this, so that everyone comes quickly to his place at the table. A little sigh from heavy-seated Schultz. But the first question

91

goes over again to Hamann: 'What were you discussing beforehand?'

'We were talking about Pinnau,' answers Hamann, and sits himself down opposite Kant.

'Gentlemen'—that's Kant again—'Bookkeeper Pinnau of the local licentiate shot himself this morning. With the esprit of a gentleman just as he lived.'

Wasianski shaken: Pinnau? And now it is known then: Pinnau, son of worthy, that is poor people, of often proven industry, who was the first to start bathing in the river Pregel, and do other things and write some pieces of poetry too—but what will become of him, where does he come from then? no room for him here; perhaps Kanter should have been able to accept him as one of his (but no-one says that, for Kanter is present) or Korff or Hippel; something of the sort is always possible; but now he had indeed gone under; so Pinnau held a pistol to his face, and was now lying in the middle of the empty office, still beneath a blackish cloud that would not settle over him.

'Why does a man like Pinnau shoot himself?' says Scheffner, and for Motherby, if that is a question, he does not realise it. Indeed, who does? Everything was going well with him, bookkeeper at the licentiate, he was getting married, six trees from Stockmar's garden were promised him. 'No professional reasons then, eh, Mr. Hamann?'

A lively conversation. That brings the cylindrical wooden dolls, skittle pins, lozenges, even the Schulz pyramid into rather too boisterous a movement. Although everything remains on its chair. One would have to be hard of hearing: then one could enjoy it just as if at a masked ball.

Kant raises his pale little face opposite unmannered Hamann, who once again has stuck his left leg with his muddy shoe on the empty chair next to him, and calls over to him: 'You know then?' And Hamann says: 'Yes,' and Schulz should at last bring his pointed blessing down on their heads.

'So,' says Kant, 'Gentlemen, let us begin the meal. Please, Head Court Chaplain!' and Schulz: ... 'Gather us daily together around your gifts, dear Lord, gather us around your throne.'

(22) *Looking at a picture*

That they did very well in the last century: voyages of discovery and the reports on them. I am thinking of Torell, de Long, Nordenskiöld and above all of the older but well-known Krusenstern, who travelled widely in the North and wrote about the oceans: such wonderful works with volumes of texts, atlases, folios of illustrations. And now I place this picture that must come from such a folio in front of me on the table.

A lithograph, coloured, a large sheet in broadside.

You see a bay, a stretch of water with little reefs, boulders and shingle, heaps of stones, which grey, reddish, sulphur yellow and green rise up out of the water. Behind, a coast rounded out by the rain or by full streams or by an exceptional high tide, now torn by some gulley, now plunging down, steep, to a flat stretch of sand, but with its slopes still high, perhaps safe enough, and there up top above the slopes and reaching right close to them a village.

Sixteen houses can be counted on this picture, there must be a few more though, and a church is there, all out of wood, and, beginning at the church over to the right as far as the point of the land a kind of headland behind which the coast then draws back and the open sea becomes visible : crosses, wooden crosses. First a whole group, fourteen or more, then a single one particularly tall with a roof from its peak to the ends of the arms, finally once more at some distance further towards the sea four such crosses, these last propped up with struts against the force of the wind.

On the sea out there a three-master which perhaps is lying at anchor. In front of it a little sailing boat, a fore-and-after or so it seems.

Pjatiza on the South coast of Russian Lapland.

So it says beneath the picture framed in four lines in a so-called light script, in capitals, that is, just formed out of thin sketching lines.

Pjatiza a village, sixteen wooden houses, a church, several crosses, on the Ter coast or perhaps already out beyond the Warsuga in Kandalakscha, I don't know. But on the White Sea anyhow, on the Kola Peninsula. There there are harbours free from ice the whole year through.

Wooden houses. Nobody who has lived in houses like this can ever forget them. You awake and you stretch yourself, let yourself breathe in and out, slowly, still with closed eyes and you feel : the house is breathing likewise and is stretching itself, it is as if it wanted to speak, and you wait for it to do so. And in the winter it seems to draw in closer around you, the walls come nearer, the roof sinks a little, closer around the warmth, nearer about your sleep. And the fine walls set out of round trunks, on the outside blackened by the storms and smooth by the sun, but already a little cracked here and there.

Not too close to one another the houses but yet not too far apart, here a house, and another and another, sixteen houses, perhaps a few more, and the church with a polygonal wooden tower and a circular tin roof. Then the crosses begin.

The man there quite small. He is going past a house and disappearing behind it. And now he can be seen again in the gap towards the next house.

There he goes. He meets a few children and stays standing. He is called Shörij, or so the children say. They ask what he is going to do now. Where he has come from no-one asks.

What sort of man is that?

He it was who put up the crosses, all the crosses which we have previously counted. The fourteen close to the church, the one tall one standing alone and the others towards the headland. What is that, a cross?

A sign. A remembrance. A memory. Something that recalls former events, things past. But so that the remembrance of that past shall be kept alive, you understand. Thus a sign of warning too, and not just against forgetfulness, against heedlessness too. That is why it must be tall and visible from afar.

We look across the whole bay and notice it from here, the single one and the others too, we can count them.

The man has gone on with the children past the next house. Shörij, say the children, when are you going to build another cross? And the man says: I am just collecting wood for the fire, help me a little.

Building crosses and lighting fires, so that's what the man does. And why?

We let him go. The children disperse among the houses and behind the wooden fences and up to the undergrowth that begins at the last houses.

A clear day. It is bright here and for months by night too. The clouds are large and powerful but very high today, the wind has plenty of space. And it goes slowly and strongly beneath the sky like a great current, silently. Only towards evening does it find a voice, who knows from where.

So the man lights fires. Towards evening. And keeps them going over night. Crosses for the day and fires for the night. Signs that can be seen from afar, signs of warning. Only that, or signs of remembrance too?

A man who lives alone but who speaks to the children and to people, although he does not know much in the language which they have here, a stranger then. But he remains here for the crosses and the fires, he has something to do and he does it. For how long already? Ten years or fifteen?

Yes, I think it must be as long ago as that.

I mean the shipwreck then in the corner westwards from the entrance into the bay which you cannot see on the picture. A Swedish or a Danish ship it was, a three-master, just as on the picture. On a stormy night, forgotten now, in a year no longer rememberd.

But month after month ships draw past here along the offshore reefs and the clearer water over the shallows on this not undangerous coast.

So the man has remained here when he pulled himself out on to the sand, he alone. And the bodies of the others he searched out on the beach, and buried them up on the heights, and raised the first crosses. Signs of remembrance.

And then he placed right on the water's edge a tall cross, a sign of warning, and now there are more and more crosses along the whole coast from the headland as far along as the village. And he must protect them against the storm and put up again those that have fallen down. And drag the wood for this from afar. And in the summer nights when the crosses are only faintly visible in the mist from the side of the sea, and in the early twilight and the dark nights after the light months he lights fires and keeps the flames burning until morning and in the winter through the day also.

The crosses I see on this picture many have also seen, travellers and then the readers of the travel books of Krusenstern and others I do not know. But I don't know if these fires are mentioned anywhere in any report, if the seafarers tell of them who come past here and are warned by them. As by the crosses.

It was profitable to write this down here. No slight gain as you will admit. It has been accomplished by a stranger who happened to come here and did not go away because something here needed to be done : with fires and crosses.

With which so much else has been done, but who thinks of that.

Take the picture from the table and hang it in front of you on your wall. So that you may see it. Sign of remembrance, sign of warning, both.

(23) *Letter from America*

Burn me, burn me, burn me, sings the old woman and turns around nice and slowly and deliberately, and now she slips off the wooden clogs from her feet—there they fly in a curve right up the fence—and she twists herself round faster and faster under the little apple-tree. Burn me, sweet sun, she sings. She has pushed up the sleeves of her blouse and swings her bare arms, and from the branches of the little tree fall little thin shadows, it is bright midday, and the old woman turns herself with little steps. Burn me, burn me, burn me.

In the house on the table lies a letter. From America. It reads:

My dear Mother,

Just to tell you we shan't be coming to see you. Only a few days now, I tell my wife, and we shall be there, and a few days more Alice, I say, and we shall be back. And it is written: honour thy Father and Mother, and although Father is dead, his grave is there, and Mother is old, I say, and if we don't go now, we shall never go. And my wife says: now listen John, she calls me John, it's lovely there, that you have told me, but that was before. A man is young or old, she says, and a young man does not know how things will be when he is old, and an old man does not know how things were in his youth. You've become something here, and you are no longer there. That's what my wife says. And she's right. You know her father signed his business over to us, and it's doing well. You can have your Mother come here, she says. But you wrote, Mother, that you cannot come, because someone must stay there as all of us have gone away.

The letter is still longer. It comes from America. And at the end stands: Your son, Jons.

It is bright midday and it is beautiful. The house is white. At the side there stands a stall. The stall too is white. And here is the garden. Just a little way down the mountain stands the next farmyard, and then comes the village alongside the river, and the road bends towards it and goes past and once again up to the river and back again and into the wood. It is beautiful. And it is bright midday. Beneath the little apple-tree the old woman turns around. She swings her bare arms. Sweet sun, burn me, burn me.

In the parlour it is cool. From the ceiling dangles a mugwort and hums with flies. The old woman takes the letter from the table, folds it together and carries it into the kitchen and on to the oven. She goes back again into the parlour. Between the two windows hangs the mirror, there in the lower left-hand corner between frame and glass there sticks a photograph. A photograph from America. The old woman takes the photo out, sits down at the table and writes on the back : That is my son Jons. And that is my daughter Alice. And beneath that she writes Erdmuthe Gauptate née Attalle. She pulls down the sleeves of her blouse and smoothes them out. A pretty white material with little blue spots. From America. She stands up, and while she is going up to the stove, she swings the photo a little in the air. When Annus von Tauroggen came then and stayed here then : it is because of her arms, he said, you don't find such white arms up there where he came from, nor here, where he then stayed. And for thirty years he spoke about them. Annus.

A man is young or old. For what after all does an old person need? The daylight wanes, the shadows become clearer, the night is no longer for sleep, the ways shorten. Just two or three ways left, finally one.

She puts the photo on the stove close to the folded letter. Then she fetches matches from the cupboard and places them by the photo. Let's boil the milk, she says, and goes out to fetch wood.

(24) *Mouse banquet*

Moise Trumpeter is sitting on the little chair in the corner of the shop. The shop is small and it is empty. Probably because the sun which is for ever coming in needs room, and the moon too. He also always comes in whenever passing by. The moon then as well. He has come in, the moon, in through the door, the shop bell has only moved once and quite quietly, but perhaps not indeed because the moon came in, but because the little mice are just running and dancing around on the thin deal boards. So the moon has come in, and Moise has said 'Good evening, moon!' and now they are both looking at the little mice.

But every day the mice act differently, now they dance this way and now that, and all that on four legs with a pointed head and a thin little tail.

'But, dear moon,' says Moise, 'that's a long way from being all, for they have too such a small body, and just think of all that's in it! But perhaps you can't understand that, and besides it doesn't change every day, but is always completely and exactly the same, and that is what I think is so very remarkable. It will of course indeed be true that you are different every day, although you nevertheless always come through the same door, and it is always dark before you have sat down here. But now just be still and watch carefully.'

You see, it's always the same.

Moise has let a crust of bread fall in front of his feet, there the little mice scurry closer inch by inch, some even sit up and sniff a little in the air. You see that's how it is. Always the same.

So there sit the two old people enjoying it all and at first do not hear at all that the shop door has been opened. Only the mice have heard it at once and are away, right away and so quickly that one can't tell where they have run to.

In the door stands a soldier, a German. Moise has good eyes, he sees: a young man, just a schoolboy, who really doesn't know at all what he wanted here now that he is standing in the door. Let's see how the Jews live, he will have thought to himself outside. But now the old Jew is sitting on his little chair, and the shop is bright with moonlight. 'Care to come in then Lieutenant?' says Moise.

The young man closes the door. He doesn't even wonder that the Jew can speak German, he just stands there, and when Moise stands up and says: 'Come then and sit yourself down, I don't have a second chair,' he says: 'Thanks I can stand,' but he steps forward a few paces into the middle of the shop and then three more paces up to the chair. And as Moise invites him again to sit down, he does so.

'Now just sit quietly,' said Moise, and leans against the wall.

The crust of bread is still lying there, and, look, there come the mice again. Just as before, not in the slightest more slowly, exactly as before, just a little at first, then a little further, sitting up and sniffing and with a tiny little wheeze which only Moise hears and perhaps the moon too. Just exactly as before.

And now they have found the crust again. A mouse banquet in a small frame, of course nothing special but not entirely an everyday occurrence all the same.

There they sit and watch. The war is already a few days old. The country is called Poland. It is quite flat and sandy. The roads are bad, and there are many children here. What else can one say about it? The Germans have come, countless hordes of them, and one is sitting here in the Jew's shop, a very young one, a milk-sop. He has a mother in Germany and a father, also still in Germany, and two little sisters. Now we'll see a bit of the world, he will be thinking, now we're in Poland, and later perhaps we'll go to England, and this Poland here is very Polish.

The old Jew leans against the wall. The mice are still gathered around their crust. When it has got a bit smaller, an older mouse-mother will take it with her back home, and the other mice will run on after.

'You know,' says the moon to Moise, 'I must be on a bit further.' And Moise in fact knows that the moon finds it uncomfortable because this German is sitting there. Just what does he want then? So Moise only says : 'Stay a little while longer.'

But at that the soldier now gets up. The mice run away from him, one really cannot say where they can all disappear to so quickly. He wonders if he should say goodbye, so stands then a moment longer in the shop, and then simply goes out.

Moise says nothing, he is waiting for the moon to

begin to speak. The mice have gone, disappeared.
Mice can do that.

'That was a German,' says the moon, 'you know of
course what these Germans are up to.' And as Moise
is still leaning as he did before against the wall and
saying nothing at all, he carries on more insistently :
'You don't want to run away, you don't want to hide
yourself, eh Moise? That was a German, that you
must have seen. Just don't tell me the young man
isn't one, or at least not a bad one. That makes no
difference any longer. When they have overrun
Poland, what will become of your people?'

'I have heard,' says Moise.

It is now quite white in the shop. The light fills the
space right up to the door in the back wall. Where
Moise is leaning, quite white, so that one thinks he is
gradually becoming more and more one with the
wall. With every word that he says. 'I know,' says
Moise, 'there you are quite right, I shall arouse the
wrath of my God.'

(25) *The first two sentences for a book on Germany.*

When the first news of the mass murders of Jews
reached the town and everyone thought they were
exaggerated (it could surely not be quite so bad, and
yet each one knew perfectly well all that in fact
happened just so—no such quite frightful numbers,
no such terrible methods and refined techniques one
heard about were exaggerated—indeed that everything had to be so, because it could not be in any
other possible way; and it was now no longer the
time to speak about it : whether there might not have

been other more charitable, more humane procedures, deportations—well, no longer now it was war, but however guaranteed sanctions with proper administration etcetera); when it was the turn of complete silence; when one had already silenced oneself completely away (who knows from what and who knows whither?), no longer traced any protest rising in one against anything, but just explained it away between an indifferently stylised joke and the solemnly damp-eyed feeling of being engaged in a struggle for destiny of mythic proportions against one's will; agreed, when it had got so far with those who ran round free in Germany and lived around under the burdensome conditions of the war; agreed, when they had come so far (which does not mean anything, for they had been so far already for a long time), if it was now going so well, as it thus was as it had always been, as it thus was, the bells were ringing—for nothing in particular : the marriage of a brain-damaged man, whose wish one had not been able to argue down in the face of his military decorations, of a First Lieutenant of the Pioneers officially liable for garrison duties but for the next few years provisionally on leave, to a nurse called Erika, who, with her own hand, had cut him down from the window-rail in the sanatorium to which he had tied himself up, and whom he strangled on his wedding-night in an indeed expected attack disturbing the balance of his mind (which also means nothing, for his official state was what is more 'being in a disturbed balance of mind' for two years, that is since he was wounded).

The latter, then, for two years, the former since when?

(26) *Valéry or The beans*

That is then a cloth, a leather, so finely tanned that it lets the light shine through, and so thick and durable that it can be stretched over both living and dead things without tearing : over a broken skeleton as over the bean-shoot, which can grow well under it and move and where possible blossom out, provided that is it finds some earth still in the pot, enough so that the roots are covered, and a little air which comes through the pores of the leather.

This cloth, yellowish-white, drawn over hooks and edges, presents here a sharp contour, here—over the bean-plant—some irregular curves, swells out nowhere, smoothly and thereby quite lightly it rests and lets itself be borne up by the silent, discreet movement of living leaves, stalks, red and white flowers.

I wanted to sketch a portrait and have not succeeded. An elderly gentleman, frail and yet firm in his flesh, who draws back with thinned veins beneath a gilt uniform, a member of the Academy with a little sword and a pretty hat on his arm. I have not succeeded, have turned too much towards the beans, to the shoot, which is a martial growth—still under a fine yellowish leather cloth that let's through the light of day.

(27) *De homine publico tractatus*

One is not equipped for life. One has one's nature, one's senses—in the town five, in the country seven. Such tools these senses—a whole forge in your ear Bayer in Vienna has called them, and elsewhere developed fauna and flora or floral fauna or vice versa, which with their full agreement you nourish and carry with you through the struggles of life; it is a pleasant feeling to be active as a complex natural living organism. Artificially and finely prepared. Says Neander, but that is not enough.

Now there are all sorts of things that come to your aid: readiness to help and respect for man in general, punishment and forced isolation for the lawbreaker, rules and regulations for the official. All there to help you find your way.

And then moral commitments. Which one feels. Inwardly. And indeed love of animals and knowledge of human nature.

Petrat is a post-office official. In Abschwangen or somewhere else, but not in Uderwangen, Uderwangen is larger. And he has his rules.

1. *Keeping office-hours*

So there sits Petrat in his office cubicle on Sunday, so the post office is shut, he is sitting at the table on his office chair with the arm-rests and the calico covering. A quiet place like pure green that comes from the trees. There he looks through the window. Everything tidied up, swept, dusted, fly-catchers renewed, outside on the little entrance steps sand strewn.

And there comes the old woman wandering along the village street, and already at the entrance to the village leaves the left-hand side to come over to the right-hand side where the post office stands at the end of the village, needs then a good four hundred metres along the whole diagonal, a hair's breadth exactness which she measures out diagonally with no respect for the famous Abschwangen pavement.

Arrives then, and the post-office is shut, closed, sand strewn, Sunday.

Let us say: this old woman is called Krepszta-kiene, the wife of Krepsztakies that is—and on a Sunday, so all in black, with shoes and the headdress with the full complement of tassels.

Petrat has been able to see her, this regular approach, he sees in her hand the letter, the other hand is a clenched fist, so that's where she has her money squeezed together. You don't make such a trip to stand in front of the door; there's no question of going away business unfinished. Petrat waits until Krepsztakiene comes to the window.

Ah, will you please, Petrat.

So Petrat proceeds to the window, opens it, slips on the catch. Today is Sunday, post-office is shut, office-hours are fixed on the door, but that won't help at all now, he knows that all by himself, Petrat, official and man.

Now whoever just thinks that there could be a struggle between duty and desire, office and friend-liness, state and individual, why he's fooling himself.

Petrat says: doors stay closed, no office-hours on sacred Sunday, have them back there in the local, but not at my place. He takes a chair, puts it through the window, outside against the house-wall, a second chair he moves from inside in front of the window, bends far out, helps Mrs. K. on to the chair outside, on to the window-sill, on to the chair inside.

Now she stands on firm ground. Petrat sits down in his official chair, the post-office remains closed, back there it is not: that would mean opening the back door, he takes the money and a stamp out of the stamp-book.

Afterwards back along the already described way. Goodbye Mrs. Krepsztakies.

2. *Retaining authority*

That is not laid down in regulations. But it is important, it concerns the dignity of the office, thus needs special care and attention, but less personal honour in this than for the state. Shall I wherever possible lick stamps for everyone?

It used to go like this: people bring their letter, place it on the table together with their money. The post-office official checks address and consigner, takes the money and produces a stamp: that is he sticks it on before the eyes of the consigner. For this consigner has officially acquired the stamp—it belongs to him. On the other hand the stamp is a seal, an official paper, even if only a small one, and you don't distribute that to just anybody. But: shall I wherever possible lick stamps for everyone?

Petrat therefore introduces: letter down, money down, tongue out. On the stretched-out tongue the stamp is dampened, Petrat only needs to raise his arm, the stamp lies gummed side open on first and middle finger. Slip off, and then of course stick on, rubber stamp, goodbye.

3. *The official has to consider himself as a servant of society*

It's easy to say state in the place of society—I just mention that. He has to consider himself stands there, we add to that: and act accordingly. Petrat acts accordingly. And considers himself as well.

That was a long time ago. Then it was heard, and those who had a newspaper read it in the newspaper, that there was now wireless, something new in the world, true voices out of the air, that is they would come from an apparatus and a gramophone horn. Something quite different from the voices in the wind which shepherd Pasnokat means, where you hear everything and nothing true. He is outside all summer long. If you want to speak to him he says : wot's that ter me?

Wireless then. And Petrat as a servant. And things don't come all that quickly as far as Abschwangen.

So Petrat has it announced : this evening wireless in the post-office, entrance free. And sticks postman Lemke with his accordion in the large cupboard. Then come the people in the evening and sit down, Petrat says : the wireless will begin shortly. And so postman Lemke plays in the cupboard, nice and clandestine it is, as if the music was coming from far off, out of the air, from Berlin, on those waves, just like Petrat said.

4. *Knowledge of human nature*

This is part and parcel of public office. Of course : principles. But what works and has an effect is done among people, with people. It is played out amongst people, just as was said. People don't stand in an account book.

Anyone who doesn't want to believe that experiences it among people. Just stand up and go among them, and best of all stay.

Petrat is sitting in the local on the eve of the Sabbath—Saturday of course—and by no means alone. Schlitzkus mine host goes up and down among his seven tables, first he, then his wife, then he stands at the bar. It is noisy in the taproom but it is peaceful, a pure peace that there is.

Petrat is telling stories, all the time keeping up the dignity of the postal services, the others listening except for teacher Laudien who is singing quietly to himself. And then the telephone rings.

Abschwangen three three three says Schlitzkus, then he listens a while, then he says : Bottke you must go home. Oh dear, says Bottke, and Petrat says something about women and men. The German woman has learnt to wait for her man. And when that Mrs. Bottke calls a second time, Bottke is still there and stays there in his seat. Perhaps he might have gone by now of course.

And now the telephone rings for the third time. At this Bottke stands up and with him Petrat. And Bottke stays standing and Petrat steps up to the telephone and says : Good evening.

Ah, I see, so you're there, you with your little stories, of course I should have thought of that, says Mrs. Bottke and says some more and wants to say some more still, but that means pushing friendliness too far for Petrat, so he says for his part (just watch the double-edges) : Mrs. Bottke, starting off quite firmly, but letting his voice die away in an obliging tone, continuing then so factually and objectively, yet at the same time a little disarmed and with it sympathetically as well (because quite unwillingly we have become a witness, witness to such a scene) : Mrs. Bottke, you haven't come to the phone in your nightdress?

No, Mrs. Bottke doesn't ring again. Mr. Bottke can stay awhile. Sit yourself down again, says Petrat.

Such matters you can only feel. Perhaps feelings

are somewhat unreliable, but it can't be helped, that's all we have to go on. If you insisted on seeing everything exactly and for yourself, just what would you start off.

In Allenburg, or maybe not in Allenburg, there was once a married couple, he squinted, she squinted, neither has seen the other ever in their lives. Have stayed together through the bad times '14, '18 and died together '24.

That's what I think.

SELECT BIBLIOGRAPHY

(A) BOBROWSKI'S WORK
1. Lyric poetry
Das Land Sarmatien, Ungekürzte Ausgabe der Bände *Sarmatische Zeit* und *Schattenland Ströme*, DTV (Munich, 1966), 127 pp. mit einem Nachwort von Horst Bienek.
Wetterzeichen, Verlag Klaus Wagenbach (Berlin, 1967), 81 pp.
Pruzzische Elegie, Sinn und Form (Berlin, 1955), Heft 4, pp. 495–501.
Some fifteen other poems and thirty epigrams have been published in various periodicals and collections.

2. Prose
Levins Mühle. Vierunddreissig Sätze über meinen Grossvater, Roman, S. Fischer Vlg (Frankfurt a.M. 1964), 295 pp.
Boehlendorff und andere, Erzählungen, Deutsche Verlags-Anstalt (Stuttgart, 1965), 97 pp.
Mäusefest und andere Erzählungen, Verlag Klaus Wagenbach (Berlin, 1965), 81 pp.
Litauische Claviere, Roman, Verlag Klaus Wagenbach (Berlin, 1967), 173 pp.
Der Mahner, Erzählungen und andere Prosa aus dem Nachlass, Verlag Klaus Wagenbach (Berlin, 1968), 69 pp.

3. Autobiographical material.
The volume *Selbstzeugnisse und Beiträge über sein*

Werk, Union Vlg (Berlin, 1967), 253 pp. includes the following:

(i) Gerhard Wolf:
     Skizze zu einer Biographie

(ii) Johannes Bobrowski:
     Mein Thema
     Lebenslauf
     Benannte Schuld—gebannte Schuld?
     Antworten auf zwei Umfragen
     Die Koexistenz und das Gespräch
     Die Deutschen und ihre östlichen Nach-
         barn
     Ansichten und Absichten
     Vom Hausrecht des Autors
     Positionsbestimmungen
     Meinen Landsleuten erzählen, was sie
         nicht wissen
     Kultur—die Vermenschlichung der Ver-
         hältnisse
     Formen, Fabel, Engagement

(iii) Hubert Faensen:
      Gedenken und Warnzeichen
      Siegfried Streller:
      Zeit und Verantwortung/Zum epischen
      Werk Johannes Bobrowskis
      Bernd Jentzsch:
      Schöne Erde Vaterland
      Gerhard Wolf:
      Motive des Lyrikers Bobrowski
      Günter Wirth:
      Dichtung als christliches Zeugnis
      Gerhard Desczyk:
      "Das ist dein Bruder, du hörst ihn"

(iv) Oskar Jan Tauschinski:
    Rede bei der Übergabe des Alma-Johanna-Koenig-Preises 1962
  Britta Titel:
    Johannes Bobrowski/Eine Studie über seine Lyrik
  Alfred Kurella:
    Laudatio bei der Verleihung des Heinrich-Mann-Preises 1965
  Carl Zuckmayer:
    Laudatio bei der Zuerkennung des Charles-Veillon-Preises 1965
  Alfred Kurella:
    In memoriam Johannes Bobrowski
  Stephan Hermlin:
    Worte am Grab
  G. Groman:
    Abschiedslicht/Eine Studie über die Werke Johannes Bobrowskis

(v) Bibliographie, Zusammengestellt von Gerhard Rostin
  Anmerkungen
  Zu den Abbildungen

5. Translations into English

Shadow Land, selected poems translated by Ruth and Matthew Mead, Donald Carroll (London, 1966), 62 pp.

Graveyard, The Sing-Swan, translated by Christopher Middleton, *Times Literary Supplement* 28.4.1961.

Holunderblüte, translated by Christopher Middleton, *Times Literary Supplement* 21.9.1962.

Also to be noted are the tributes *To Johannes Bobrowski* by Christopher Middleton in *Times*

Literary Supplement 21.9.1962, and *In memoriam Johannes Bobrowski* by Matthew Mead *Neue Zürcher Zeitung* 16.10.1965.

Bobrowski himself published translations from the Czech of Konstantin Biebl, from the Russian of Boris Pasternak and S. Marschak.

(B) SECONDARY LITERATURE

The majority of the secondary literature is short and has appeared in various periodicals and newspapers, many in East Germany. Apart from the essays, etc., listed in *Selbstzeugnisse* (see above) two complete volumes have appeared:

Sigfrid Hoefert, *West-Östliches in der Lyrik Johannes Bobrowskis*, Verlag UNI-Druck (Munich, 1966), 72 pp.

Gerhard Wolf, *Johannes Bobrowski. Leben und Werk. Schriftsteller der Gegenwart* Deutsche Reihe 19, Volk und Wissen Volkseigener Vlg (Berlin, 1967), 123 pp.

Other articles of interest include:

Anon, 'The pastoral folkworld', *Times Literary Supplement* 21.9.1962, p. 729.

Anon, Ground Down (*Levins Mühle*), *Times Literary Supplement* 14.1.1965, p. 21.

Anon, 'Past Impersonal' (*Boehlendorff und andere Erzählungen*), *Times Literary Supplement* 30.9.1965, p. 846.

Anon, 'The East End of Guilt' (*Litauische Claviere*), *Times Literary Supplement* 22.9.1966, p. 872.

Hans Peter Anderle, 'Johannes Bobrowski. Porträt. Literaturhinweise. Levins Mühle (Auszug)'. In:

Mitteldeutsche Erzähler, Verlag Wissenschaft und Politik (Cologne, 1965), pp. 184–190.

Manfred Bieler, 'Sarmatische Zeit' (*Sarmatische Zeit* and *Schattenland Ströme*), *Neue Deutsche Literatur* 1962 Heft 9 September, pp. 141–144.

Horst Bienek, 'Striche zu einem Porträt', *Merkur* 1966 (20) (2) Nr. 215, pp. 133–137.

Bernhard Böschenstein, 'Immer zu benennen', Mit Text und Kommentar von Johannes Bobrowski. In: *Doppelinterpretationen*, ed. Hilde Domin, Athenäum Vlg (Frankfurt a.M., 1966), pp. 101–105.

Patrick Bridgwater, 'The Poetry of Johannes Bobrowski', *Forum for Modern Language Studies* 1966 (2) (4), pp. 320–334.

Anni Carlsson, 'Johannes Bobrowski und Klopstock', *Neue Zürcher Zeitung* 15.1.1966.

Günther Cwojdrak, *Litauische Claviere. Die Weltbühne*, Berlin 13.7.1966, Nr. 28, pp. 881–883.

Jerry Glenn, 'An Introduction to the Poetry of Johannes Bobrowski', *The Germanic Review* 1966 (41) (1), pp. 45–56.

Walter Gross, 'Zeit ohne Angst—Zu den Gedichten von Johannes Bobrowski', *Reformatio* (Zürich, 1965), Nr. 10, pp. 603–616.

Michael Hamburger, 'Aufruf des Dichters', *Merkur* 1966 (20) (2), pp. 131–132.

Michael Hamburger, 'Foreword to Shadow Land. Selected Poems of Johannes Bobrowski, Donald Carroll (London, 1966), pp. 7–9.

Gerhard Hartung, 'Johannes Bobrowski', *Sinn und Form* 1966 Heft 4, pp. 1189–1217.

Rolf Haufs, 'Der Lyriker Johannes Bobrowski',

Gewerkschaftliche Monatshefte (Cologne, 1963), Nr. 12 December, pp. 739–746.

Sigfrid Hoefert, 'Überliefertes und schöpferische Gestaltung in Bobrowskis *Die Seligkeit der Heiden*', *Seminar* 1968 (4) (1) Spring, pp. 57–66.

Karl August Horst, 'Johannes Bobrowski und der epische Realismus', *Merkur* 1964 Heft 10/11 Nr. 200, October-November, pp. 1080–1082.

Peter Jokostra, 'Dichtung gegen Angst und Tod', *Eckart Jahrbuch* 1962/1963, pp. 205–208.

Peter Jokostra, 'Sections of: 'Bobrowski und andere', *Die Chronik des Peter Jokostra*, Langen-Müller Vlg (Munich, 1967).

Hermann Kähler, '*Levins Mühle*. Bobrowskis Roman', *Sinn und Form* 1965 (3–4), pp. 631–636.

Werner Liersch, 'Aus der Hand der Vergangenheit' (On *Levins Mühle*), *Neue Deutsche Literatur* 1965 Heft 2, pp. 146–149.

Werner Liersch, 'Das Flüchtige fest machen' (On *Boehlendorff* and *Mäusefest* collections), *Neue Deutsche Literatur* 1965 Heft 12, pp. 139–144.

Joachim Müller, 'Der Lyriker Johannes Bobrowski—Dichtung unserer Zeit', *Universitas* 1968 (23) (12), pp. 1301–1311.

Jost Nolte, 'Zum Tode Johannes Bobrowskis', *Die Welt* 3.9.1965.

Hans-Jürgen Schmitt, 'Magie und Rhythmus. Zum Gedicht *Trauer um Jahnn* von Johannes Bobrowski', *Frankfurter Allgemeine Zeitung* 15.7.1966.

Jean-Claude Schneider, 'Hommage à Bobrowski', *La Nouvelle revue Française*, 1966 (14) (163) July, pp. 112–117.

Peter Paul Schwarz, 'Freund mit der leisen Rede'.

Zur Lyrik Johannes Bobrowskis', *Der Deutsch-unterricht* 1966 (18) (2) May, pp. 48–65.

Manfred Seidler, 'Bobrowski, Klopstock und der antike Vers'. In: *Lebende Antike. Symposium für Rudolf Sühnel*, Erich Schmidt Vlg (Berlin, 1967), pp. 542–554.

Eric Standaert, 'Johannes Bobrowski. Een inleiding tot zijn poëzie', *Diagram voor progressieve literatur* 1964 (2) (1), pp. 35–58.

Helmut Ullrich, 'Entdeckung, eines Dichters. Ein Porträt von Johannes Bobrowski'. In: *Welt-offenheit als Lebensprinzip, Begegnungen mit christlichen Kunstschaffenden in der DDR*, Union Vlg (Berlin, 1962), pp. 152–156.

Klaus Wagenbach, 'Johannes Bobrowski', *Jahresring* 1966/1967, pp. 310–313.

H. M. Waidson, 'Bobrowski's *Levins Mühle*', In: *Essays in German Language, Culture and Society*, Edited by S. S. Prawer, R. Hinton Thomas and L. Forster, The Institute of Germanic Studies (London, 1969), pp. 149–159.

Jürgen P. Wallmann, 'Johannes Bobrowski: *Levins Mühle*,' *Neue Deutsche Hefte* 1965 Nr. 103 January-February, pp. 151–153.